THE RHYME
OF THE
AG-ED MARINESS

1972

THE RHYME
OF THE
AG-ED MARINESS

The Last Poems of
LYNN LONIDIER

Edited by Janine Canan
Preface by Jerome Rothenberg
Photographs by Fred Lonidier

STATION HILL

BARRYTOWN, LTD.

Published by Station Hill / Barrytown, Ltd.
in Barrytown, New York 12507.

E-mail: publishers@stationhill.org
Online catalogue: http://www.stationhill.org

Station Hill Arts is a project of The Institute for Publishing Arts, Inc., a not-for-profit, federally tax exempt organization in Barrytown, New York, which gratefully acknowledges ongoing support for its publishing program from the New York State Council on the Arts.

Typeset and design by Susan Quasha
Cover design by Susan Quasha
Photographs of Lynn Lonidier on front cover (1987) and on pages 2,6,109-112 by Fred Lonidier

"Lesbian Heaven" was previously published in *Poetry: USA* (Berkeley CA, 1993.)

Library of Congress Cataloging-in-Publication Data
Lonidier, Lynn.
        The rhyme of the ag-ed mariness : the last poems of Lynn Lonidier / edited by Janine Canan ; preface by Jerome Rothenberg ; photographs by Fred Lonidier.
                p. cm.
        ISBN 1-58177-052-9 (alk. paper)
        1. Lesbians–Poetry. 2. Feminisim–Poetry. I. Title: Rhyme of the aged mariness. II. Canan, Janine. III. Title.
PS3562.O535 R49 2000
811'.54–dc21   00-031208

Manufactured in the United States of America

Contents

1964

Preface

Five years after her death, Lynn Lonidier remains—for me, for us
—one of that company of poets who has shaped an image-of-the-
world we now can recognize as true & true in ways we hadn't known
before she showed them to us. The proof of that world for her—as
for so many of her mentors & her fellows—lies in the poem, the
writing, where she works as maker (poet) of the myth (the story
told, retold, created). As with those others too, a liberated word or
series of such liberated words dominates & leads the mind toward
meaning, seeing. In her work, as I read it, that word lies in the
"lesbian estate" of an earlier title, from where it comes into her
other writings. It functions for her much as the word "jew" once did
for me or, more clearly still, for our friend Edmond Jabès—not the
"whole story" (ours or hers) but a key for unlocking the "whole
story." In this way Jabès could speak of "jew" (the word & what was
signaled by it) as "an obsession for me...like the word 'God.'" And
in that way too, Lonidier might have spoken of "lesbian" or those
words akin to "lesbian" that she freed up & that freed her up in
turn.

I think it is important to foreground this for her—even so early in
this pre-face. For hers is no sentimental accounting—as legitimate
as that may be—of a life lived, but the recognition of a truly psychic,
therefore mythic, space that guides her exploration of the full (re-
peat: the full) range of our experience as sentient beings. In *A Les-
bian Estate,* then, she has us "picture a lesbian estate on the cliffs
of California where doors open green and bodies open blue." The
exploration of that estate begins with a series of poems, an "open-
ing dream" in which the word "hermaphrodite" predominates—a
world, she further writes, where "There is god there is man   and
there are monsters." Within parameters like those—& in the setting
of a young girl "little angel face reading about hermaphrodites   Sun-
day morning January 18 1970"—the poem explodes into a series of
linked images, imaginal & real at once

Where witches walk   beasts and bad smells are let out the shadows
of their centipede tags   Hoop snakes   tails in mouths   jump out of
their skirts   toll uphill scarin' the slithers   out of villagers
The villagers scatter like stars

When my hermaphrodite meets your hermaphrodite   hermaphrodite
will turn from hermaphrodite (body kiss of body)   Heaven turn
around and   song stand still   when Hermaphrodite Your meets
Hermaphrodite My

Here we are already—typically—into an area beyond the confessional, an area in which dream & invention will link with inherited mythological figures—the Greek Tiresias, say, who knew both male & female, who will speak again through her, when she proclaims for both of them:

I too
had seen   two snakes   ringing halos through the grass The Physique
of Mixed Form Light   LIGHT

From here too she can invent/imagine her way to places her mind now allows her — places where "women think their centers are jelly fish" & where the thought gives rapid rise to other thoughts:

Look at a jellyfish called the moon a jellyfish is invisible
If you run your fingers through water you might catch one   It won't
hurt   It is like holding your heart in your hand or a breast A
handful of milk   shirking and winking like a giant teardrop that
any minute might harden   in a kleenex

It was with those poems in *A Lesbian Estate* that I first came to a clear recognition of what the power was that drove her work. I had met her earlier during my own first visits to San Diego and had known her then in the circle of Pauline Oliveros & other friends & artists there. But by the time of *A Lesbian Estate,* she was settled into San Francisco, where she worked with the new Women's Building, taught school with great enthusiasm (& later anxieties), and was a friend to some who were my own key friends in poetry & who brought me, as she did too, into new territories of mind & spirit. The cover of A Lesbian Estate was by Jess—a great wraparound collage by the artist who for many years had shared a life & art with Robert Duncan. I came to know Lynn again as a part of Robert and Jess's world—to read her anew as the maker of a nascent fiction, as magical as life itself. Theirs was a "Hermetic Circle," she wrote, in which "Robert and Jess play Kipling / upon the crank phonograph," and she was kind enough to see me as a part of that—at least in her own version. I remember her there during the days of Robert's dying & her own departure (twice) into the bourne from which no traveler returns. And following *A Lesbian Estate,* her next books, *Woman Explorer* and *Clitoris Lost,* showed her at her most developed—a writer in the world & moving thru it with a sense of high adventure & of wonder.

All these qualities come back in the present work—assembled as her "last poems" in the aftermath of suicide & loss. The long title piece—completed earlier as "lesbian—ecological opera"— brings with it a sense both of culmination & of a new beginning & a reaching out. For hers is now a global project—in the opening poems of this book an attempt to overcome limitations of language & culture with a leap (by fits & starts) into a second language (Spanish), and—in its theatrical coda a complex weaving of history, ecology, & ritual, in which the lesbian mythos (the hermetic/hermaphroditic struggle & progression of the contraries) becomes, in Robert Duncan's words, the dream of everyone, everywhere. However incomplete these gathered works may *be,* they point powerfully to where the poetry was taking her & to the greater fullness that we can only now imagine.

In that imagining, then, hers was the final voice that came to me, some years ago, when I was writing a poem called "Seedings," initiated by a dream in which Robert Duncan, himself dead several years then, appeared & led me into an improvisation of a poem about a paradise of vanished friends & poets. The last to appear there – but with her name unspoken—was Lynn Lonidier, with whom (as "lately fallen ghost") I entered into a discourse that consisted of her words as well as mine. She or her surrogate was there for me—"hermaphroditic in the shadow of / the phallic altar"—& gave me words to bring the poem to closure:

> there is god (she says)
> & man & there are monsters
> leading the way to death   among the friends who wait her presence

those who have lived a life of poetry
whom we will only see once
in that final moment when we join them
before the chill sets in
the bliss of language lost to us
forever   drifting
like mindless phantoms
empty voices
without our verbs & nouns

Here we would be wrong, of course, in thinking that the bliss of language–her language as the case in point—was already lost to us, when it does in fact persist, as in the pages of this book, where it takes life again through our reading of it. But it is her voice throughout that overshadows ours, her vision & creation dominant —for all of which I am forever grateful.

Jerome Rothenberg
New York City
September 1998

Introduction

This collection gathers together the last poems of Lynn Lonidier. It contains all the poems she is known to have written between the publication of her fifth poetry collection *Clitoris Lost* in 1989, and her death at age 56 in 1993. In the dozen boxes of manuscripts and papers Lynn left behind, I found a collection of bilingual poems which she had previously called *Spanish Immersion*, renamed *The Pocho Kid: La Language Bandida*; and *The Rhyme of the Ag-ed Mariness*, a libretto for a "lesbian-ecological opera," which she had long spoken of writing. From our mutual publisher Paul Mariah, I had already received a copy of the last poems Lynn was working on—"Til Years Let Me Grow Wiser," "Lesbian Heaven", and "Quest"—poems she was still revising at the time of her death.

Lynn was a striking woman. Tall, lanky, blond with blue eyes, she typically wore pants, sometimes sun glasses or a broad-rimmed hat. Shy yet bold, highly sensitive, she projected an image both elegant and eccentric. Lynn Lonidier was a true poet. Her writing was stunningly original, her imagination seemingly limitless. In her work unusual sentence structures and elaborate musical patterns—classical, yet jazzy thematic variations—abound. Lonidier had a flawless sense of rhythm. A master word wielder, her lines are full of plays and puns. Intensely energetic, her voice is tinged with a vast and strangely fulfilling sense of humor. Passionately and unequivocally feminist, consistently dedicated to the unprivileged, Lonidier's poetry brims with anger and irony, yet overflows with loving tenderness. In the end she was perhaps a romantic, her poems startlingly open-hearted, charged with ecstasy and visionary consciousness—a woman-centered yet universal vision of beauty, love and intelligence.

Lynn was born in Lakeview, Oregon, on April 22, 1937. Her father was a hot-tempered sawyer and trade unionist of Cajun/English descent; her mother, the daughter of a musical and socialist Swedish family, was a violinist and violin teacher. Lynn began to study cello when she was five. At age nine she moved with her parents and younger brother to Oroville, California. At twelve she wrote her first poem:

> Once there was a little boy
> Who courted the fabulous Helen of Troy.
> He was so short
> He wore some stilts to tower above
> The Fair Maiden So—.

Lynn played cello in the Oroville String Quartet, the Oroville Community Orchestra, and the Chico State College Orchestra. From Chico State, she transferred in 1954 to San Francisco State College, where she studied music and writing, majored in Education, and again played cello in the orchestra. In 1957 she graduated, and received her Elementary Teaching Credential.

To her parents' great disappointment, Lynn abandoned the cello in order to concentrate on writing poetry. For a few years she taught elementary school in Oroville, but after her father's death she returned to San Francisco. There she became active in Poets in the Schools, and helped coordinate The Pegasus Program affiliated with the Poetry Center of San Francisco State, which encouraged school children to write and publish poetry, and use audio-visual equipment in performance. Lynn loved working with children, and edited several chapbooks of children's poems, including *Blue Door I, II and III.*

Lynn met avant-garde composer Pauline Oliveros in the '50s, in the San Francisco State Orchestra where Pauline played horn. In 1966 Lynn moved into Pauline's home in Oakland. Pauline was now director of the Tape Music Center at Mills College. In 1967 the Berkeley Free Press published Lynn's first book, *Po Tree*, a lively 42-page collection of experimental poetry illustrated by Lynn and the Wong sisters. When Pauline accepted a teaching position at the University of California in San Diego, Lynn and Pauline put on a farewell all-night Tapethon in a San Francisco loft. Pauline played all of her electronic music and Lynn performed various light pieces. Their performance of "Jar Piece" was later recorded on Cadandian with Lynn's graphics. Lynn and Pauline moved to Encinitas, and later to Leucadia in southern California. They performed together at the University of California in San Diego, at The Electric Circus In New York City; and in 1970 traveled together to the

Osaka World Fair, where Pauline performed and Lynn filmed. In 1970 Lynn wrote her first novella *Candy's Cane* (unpublished), and through her Tenth Muse Press published her second poetry collection, *The Female Freeway*.

In the early '70s Lynn, now in her mid-thirties, moved to Seattle to live with her mother, and attend graduate school in Education at the University of Washington. She received a Master of Arts in Media in 1975. With other teachers she embarked on what proved to be a joyous journey to Mexico, which she filmed on Super 8 and later described in *Woman Explorer*. She traveled to Peru, where she visited Macchu Picchu, and wrote the "Quipus Diary," which was published in her last book, *Clitoris Lost*. About this time she wrote her first novel, *The Nursery*, which was never published.

After five years in Seattle, Lynn was eager to move back to Francisco. She bought a cottage in the Mission District and completed another novel, *Sacrificial Lambs,* which was also never published. In 1976 Lynn co-edited the anthology, *Poetry from Violence*. Diana Press in Oakland published one of her stories in their anthology, *The Lesbians Home Journal: Stories from The Ladder*. And in 1977 Paul Mariah's Manroot Press published Lonidier's third collection of poetry (written between 1970 and 1973 in Seattle), *A Lesbian Estate.*

A large and handsome 83-page book with a striking cover by collage artist Jess Collins, *A Lesbian Estate* received strong critical acclaim and soon sold out. Jana Harris responded in the *Poetry Flash*: "Lonidier...may well be to the 1970s what Gertrude Stein was to the 1920s." "Lonidier's poems take the reader on a circular voyage by air, ocean, and imagination," wrote Judy Thrall in *13th Moon*. "Cranky, intense, direct, filled with humor and sarcasm, these unpunctuated prose poems become a world...," said Ron Silliman in the *San Francisco Review of Books*. In Canada Judith Crewe, reviewing for *Body Politic*, claimed: "[Like Ginsberg and Wieners] Lonidier's style...operates at the frontiers of consciousness, though her themes and thought-patterns are totally female." And in *The Village Voice*, Jill Johnston summed it up: "Lynn is probably a reincarnated Emily Dickinson."

In 1979 The Painted Bride Quarterly Press of Philadelphia published Lonidier's handsome fourth collection of poetry, *Woman Explorer*. The 171- page collection included "The Lost Land of Quintana Roo," "The

Calmecac," "The Return to the Lost Land of Quintana Roo," "The Book of Women (After reading Susan Griffin's *Women and Nature*)," "Ladyland Ownerlord", and the essay "Poet's Pilgrimage to the Pyramids of Mexico," Now living and teaching in San Francisco's Spanish-speaking Mission District, Lynn joined Mission Alliance for a Popular Culture, and became interested in the writing of bilingual poetry. That same year, after a long bout of cancer with Lynn at her side, Lynn's mother died.

Lynn was a passionate and unflinching feminist. Gender themes moved powerfully through all her work. In the '80s she began to call herself an "anarcha-feminist." A "Founding Mother" of The San Francisco Women's Building, she devoted two years to finding a building for women's cultural events—although later her reading there from one of her novels incited a minor riot among offended feminists. Lynn was often frustrated by conservatism in the arts as well as society at large, and was particularly disappointed when the Bay Area Women's Philharmonic refused to perform her "Flying Symphony," a theater piece created especially for the new all-women orchestra, in which the players were to whirl on stage in long rainbow-colored dresses. In 1982 she wrote "A Lesbian Compendium for Leading the Nation down the Valentine Path," another work which was never published.

Though from time to time engaged in provocative debates with other artists, Lynn was a close friend of some of the most original American artists of her time: poets Robert Duncan and Jerome Rothenburg, artist Jess Collins, composer Pauline Oliveros, filmmakers Allie Light and Irving Saraf. She was devoted to her cousin, San Francisco poet Karen Brodine, who died in 1989, and to her brother, documentary photographer Fred Lonidier. Lynn was a loyal friend to many lesser known women artists as well. In 1983 she created for poet Noni Howard a performance piece entitled "Body Altar," which was enacted by Howard and Lonidier at San Francisco's Valencia Rose. I myself met Lynn in in the Spring of that same year at a party at Susan Griffin's sister Joanna's house, where Lynn, then working on *Clitoris Lost*, expressed an intense interest in my recent travels to Lesbos and Crete. Soon afterward Lynn discovered my little-known book *Shapes of Self*, promptly invited Robert Duncan to her home to hear some of my poems, and warmly introduced my work to her publisher Paul Mariah, who subsequently published my next book, *Her Magnificent Body*.

Lynn and I became good friends. We collaborated on a recording of my poem "Our Lady," read to a haunting composition by Lynn on synthesizer. When I requested some of Lynn's poems for my anthology, *She Rises like the Sun: Invocations of the Goddess by Contemporary American Women Poets,* she gave them to me in a folder on which she had written: "Janine, these are the final versions (virgins) of these poems." Lynn inhabited a world of poetry in which poems were living presences. She crafted each one with painstaking devotion. Her presentations of them were always intense. At Rutgers University on the East-coast book tour for the anthology, her rhythmically mesmerizing reading of "Swinging Goddess—Sally Ride; First American Woman Astronaut" roused the young students to unforgettable rapture.

In the '80s, Lynn was also involved in the completion of a quartet of "sexual minority novels," which she had been writing in the stream-of-consciousness tradition of Joyce and Stein since the '70s. The four novels, *The Banana Lady, The Hanged Man, A Very Faeire Tale,* and *Phantom of the Organ,* were never published, though they were shown to many publishing houses. In 1989 Manroot published Lonidier's beautiful self-designed *Clitoris Lost, A Woman's Version of the Creation Myth (A Take-off on John Milton's Ordering of a Heaven, Earth, and Hell),* 160 rainbow-colored pages in a computer-imaged cover depicting two women in lively conversation in the Palace of Knossos at Crete. But *Clitoris Lost,* Lonidier's response to Milton's *Paradise Lost,* was lost on the critics, not only those of the malestream, but even those of the avant-garde, feminist and gay communities.

In 1990 Lynn, now active in a group called Mother Courage, was also studying Spanish and writing a series of bilingual poems which she originally called *Spanish Immersion*, but later changed to *Pocho Poems (pocho* being a Mexican slang term for emigrants to the United States). She finally called these quasi-bilingual poems, sometimes spoken in a "stolen language," *The Pocho Kid: La Language Bandida.* In 1991 she traveled to Argentina in order to visit the poet Ilse Kornreich, and attend the International Women Writers Conference. Finally completing her long-envisioned opera libretto (with notes for music), Lynn dedicated her masterpiece to Ilse Kornreich, "valiant sailor of the Southland." A feminist revision of Coleridge's "The Rime of the Ancient Mariner," Lonidier's opera was named "The Rhyme of the Ag-ed Mariness: A Lesbian-Ecological Opera."

In 1991, Lynn was laid off from her longstanding elementary school teaching position—which had always meant a great deal to her. This blow, along with the accumulated disappointments she had experienced over the years in love as well as in work, plunged Lynn into a deep midlife depression. She never fully recovered. In 1991, and again in 1993 Lynn was hospitalized at St. Francis Hospital in San Francisco. There another patient aptly wrote these lines about her: *Pain in all four corners, courage at the core, beauty in every fold....* On May 18, 1993, Lynn left the hospital, and was later found dead from an apparently intentional fall from a cliff onto a San Francisco beach.

Thanks to her friend, the poet Noni Howard, all of the Lynn Lonidier manuscripts are now housed at the San Francisco Public Library James Hormel Gay and Lesbian Center, and Lynn Lonidier's name has been added to the San Francisco Women's Building. Films and tapes are in the possession of her brother, documentary photographer Fred Lonidier, Professor of Visual Arts at the University of California in San Diego. *Clitoris Lost* is available from Small Press Distribution in Berkeley, California.

Janine Canan, EDITOR

I

The Pocho Kid:

La Language Bandida

Bernal Hill

A tree-laced road leads to radar
screens overlying the Mission.
Morning sun timbres the bay—
Oakland—Berkeley—Mt. Tam—
in my breathtaking eye.

Two hawks cavort on Bernal Hill,
between three crows cawwing
and one starling darting. The hawks
may be young peregrines,
their white breasts speckled,
large dots on the undersides of
greytan wingtips.
¿Qué hacen en la ciudad?
I am with my dog.

The pair of hawks sail overhead,
dizzying me, circling us—
and disappear as soon as
we head along the trail.

Bluesky afternoon,
I am "la maestra," a penguin walking
school children-pilgrims.
One of the children cries, "Look up!"
*Mientras espías and hatchetmen
take breath*, the child has spied
a hawk just like the ones I'd
sited: ¡Peregrino! "Pilgrim"
is another word for
"peregrine" in Spanish.
"Looks like a cross,"
a second child announces.

Multicolored children of the Mission
ooh and ahh while signals against
nature drone metal membranes of
criminal radar screens overlying

distant clamor and chatter of
culturas diversidades de la Misión.
Cyanide-laced thinkers y hitmen de
milicia—take away aura
of reverencia de
sacred breath.

Cingcong* Singsong Goddess Poem:

*To the Guerrilla Girls on East and West
coasts, who have been protesting lack
of representation of women artists in
America's museums and galleries*

New York's got the Empire State Building,
why can't we have King Kong? I saw him
from the Bay Bridge one night on top of
a San Francisco skyscraper, blinking his
red eyes, flicking his fey wrist at the fog,
diverting cars off an ongoing, winged vision.
What're the odds of a local sculptoress
persuading The National Undoingment of the Arts
to pay Her to put one up there? King Kong
would enhance the city 'scape and Up the Pyramid
Building by One. Mighty Joe Young tilting
at wind and millwhite briefs of cases winding
in & around & trashing the daily, dark downtown.

At the top o' Nordstrom's spiral staircase,
tourists could pay to enter a chrome dome where
they keyboard King Kong to do computerized
gyrations and corporate escalations to the sky,
observe his earthquake chest pounding up cement,
read storm fronts off his fur ends, roll
his eyes at the tickering stocks, marquee
his low brow with Clairol blondes he's
programmed to ogle, blow smoke outa a cigar he's
chompin' to let ashes out on the City of Love
—a true art (advertising stogies) object—
transcending New York/L.A. art scenes
by leaps, while bound.

Urgency of alternatives 'midst 49er football
chumps and tinygiants' unbuilt new stadium

attempts to gobble up Downtown with the egos
of ants: let's make King Kong female: Goddess
Kongess—a gargantuan guerrilla stance of
towering feminist ideals spanning the Grand
Lady with the gargoyle** on her back. Largessa
bandida novices of anarchAfeminist voice
making Goddess Kongess's Caduceus of Caring
N U M E R A   U N A !!!—making me collide
with excitement, starting writing this poem
on the Female Freeway, hurtling from one kind
of gorilla to another.

*Pronounced "King Kong."
**A sculpture placed on the Bay Bridge to ward
off earthquakes and other evils.

Chingos Mingos; Genesis: Mission.
Mission Genesis

Otra Vez, Otra Basic

Mi mejor amiga en San Francisco es
secretaria por abogados de latinos.
Ella se fué.
My best friend in San Francisco is
a secretary for lawyers of Latins.
She quits and trabaja como tenedora de libros
por un centro de artistas.
She quits and catches up on accounting
and other things for an art center
for caciques consentidos y sus niñeras,
for nuturing macho administrators and
macho administrator tenders.
¡Ella se fué!
She quits
and is hired by Universidad de California.
¡Una secretaria
ahora y siempre!
Currently forever!

Dulcamara Death

Should "bollo maimónde dolor" be translated "sad round cake" or
"roundcake of sadness"?

I learned from an El Salvadorean that the word "gordo" as applied
to children means "prized dear" "precious one."
But "gordo" applied to a groan female means "fat."
I am against looks-labeling,
but my boss es gorda.
Gorda grande.

A gorda grande buffoon.
I say this not to begrudge work but to list
injusticias: *grievances:*

Uno: Summer months she's had the water fountain turned off
       that the nursery uses. I ask why. She says because the
       nursery teacher can't keep the children from playing in the
       fountain. So why should children be denied their daily quota
       of drinking water because their teacher can't control them?
       I complain to the school nurse. She says: "It's just as well.
       If they drink out of the fountain they may be getting lead in
       their systems." Children find a way: They're drinking out of
       the wash basin.

Dos: For months Gorda doesn't get the outside light changed
       that the neighborhood children broke. Come November,
       parents, children and teachers are staggering around an
       almost totally darkened facility. I tell her I won't work the
       shift without lights. Bocanada gets them fixed.

Tres: Last spring's windstorm, two huge tree limbs broke
       from an aged douglas fir tree stretched over the play
       yard. They plunged into other branches—lodging
       precariously. I reminded her and reminded her to have
       tree fellers remove them. She let children play under
       those hanging limbs well into summer—until I tattled
       on gross boss to her boss: tiny boss. The thunder of those
       sawed branches hitting the cement playground sounded
       like her body leveling the children into Pie Dough Land.

Maneras de bufón my boss keeps bags of cookies for herself
in her drawers Con las manos de bufón she reaches for dulces
en las formas de vidas de niños—candy in the shapes of children's
lives—to add to her faldas. *¡O Venga Cruelsweet Death!*

Escribo en Español

Writing in Spanish
tan bien como:
as well as
en Inglés is
quadruple la complexidad,
doble the dream.

El Arriero Del Coche

You've heard of a musketeer. In Español, an "arriero"
is a "Muleteer," the closest English word I can find
to the driver of a coach, other than "coachwoman."
The arriera describes her daughters as mules with tears,
and gives her son rein to head home Thanksgiving Day.
"You Will Not Be Moved" is in all of you.
Spanish Rose visited by Romans.

Your apartment is an arena for a golden chariot
drawn by four different-colored horses.
Cochera holds reign, and three children take off
in every direction. Over the rio and through
the bosque to 14th Street and into the sky you go,
Mother and Child and Child and Child, galloping,
galloping, galloping: Four Horsemen of the Apocalypse
with a tarot deck in the coach. Ghost of your
mother riding shotgun in back.

Is it a stagecoach or a pumpkin? It's a hybrid ride,
transporting gold pieces across the barrio,
the brightness of the body through the dark hills
of Battery Street, and turning into laughter at night
like the white witch with the turning dog and swirling
cat laughing at your side. The Laughing Lady of Playland
is what it is like to lift off an evening with you
while my house falls to the ground. We're a pair of
roughriders imbibing in golden grub, swigs of liquid
silver, me listening to your hairy stories; you
wondering if your last daughter left home for
the night or forever.

Raising a family is of a sudden landing at a racetrack
with the Marks (X) brothers, the boys at home'on street
corners, moving in Spanish passed the naming, into
the dominion of epic where words turn toward

the sun—the four horsemen—Tina and her three charges
are electric together—tarot cards turning brilliant
rubric, formulating fiery heavens, generating heat
and moisture over a breathing landscape where
humanidad es el rey.

When humanity is king, cuando cada palabra es embraced,
when out of the mouths of babes rolls the sun and
the family is still a squeaking, gilded chariot
ridden to the mewling tune of The Lone Ranger:
"Giddy-up, giddy-up, giddy-up-up-up," Tonto, never
stupid but decidedly dizzy stakes claim to the sides
of buildings, sprouting poetry, renaming the town
where you planted your feet on the floorboards
and routed in the cries of life, "Fogtown"————
"El Nublado"————"the sun heartleaping on
fragments of clouds"————"tarot cards handspringing
in a dream toward you."

After Meeting A Dream Recorder

"Boxes? Boxes!" I uttered to the heavyset woman writer
I'd traveled to meet. "I'm not interested in boxes!"
I listed women artists who'd done boxes to this literate
woman whose old dog only walked sideways like a crab
around, around the house. I awoke from dreaming,
thinking, "I'm not interested in boxes, putting things
in them and calling them a vagina."

I awoke, thrilled I'd met someone I could maybe love
and talk to, and thought, "I'm not interested in boxes
I could call a dream," I wished I'd spoken to the woman
whose dog I'd dreamed only walked crabways sidewise in
a house around a box. A house I could put things in and
call, "Meeting Someone I Could Talk To and, Perchance,
Love, crabwise sideways.

Sol Ankle Dazzle in the Department of Bilinguals

Why do you sell rain to the power-trippers who speak
another language deepening into drought?
Come be a teacher again with children.
Your life will be shorter, but sweeter,
con niños. I hear you were espiritu

with the dissenting hoarders making everything
foreign, out of touch with your own.
I get angry as you say you don't want to discuss
bilingual philosophia with me anymore. You put me away
from children of your mother's tongue.

Is being with the clicking tongues of powered adults
—before your people turn away—(Come back!)—easier?
I'm asking you to translate this into Spanish,
por mi, por favor, to see if it makes sense to you,
Yaqui!

Y tú, feather-wasted dancer with treeseed rattle
thonged just above each foot. You, too, brutal?—
from fear of the old repeat of blondes capturing
darkhaired pajarahermosas in a poem, a nightmare entitled
  "Department Bedzzlement." Mirrored smoke.
Come back! Be dead or be dazzled. Easier to *Be*.

¿Que lengua son occasiones politicales monstrositiosos?

The "Go For" Poem

I wouldn't have named my dog "Black Beauty"
even though, as a child, I loved the novel
about the horse, Black Beauty. Issues of beauty
are loaded for me. However, I agreed to take
this dog from a family who had just had a new baby
and couldn't handle a puppy, a baby and another child.
The other child, a six year old boy who is black,
named this puppy, "Black Beauty"—and is haunted
by losing her, I'm sure—and some of his identity,
given he was adopted into a white family.

In honor of the boy, I've kept the dog's name.
Dog owners compliment her shiny coat and swiftness,
and often remark on her beauty before they know
her name. They always want to know what I feed her.
I feed her what they feed their dogs.
Never have I seen a dog so resembling the loyalty,
speed and sleekness of that wonder horse leaping over
longago fences and fields of child dreams of my youth.

My other dog was found by a friend on a road
in a rainstorm. This woman named the puppy, "Sappho."
I adopted Sappho and took her where I live
in the Hispanic part of San Francisco.
An overeater, she has tendency to run off,
scavenge for food. Can you see me running
after her, calling, "Here Sappho! Here Sappho!"
in a neighborhood where Spanish-speaking men
sometimes go looking for gays to beat up or kill?

Two assumptions have been made in one tail.
Do adult Hispanic males know Sappho the Poet?
Did the mother or father read the *Black Beauty*
story to their adopted son of a different race?

More likely, he saw a watered-down version of
Black Beauty on TV and intuited his identity
by naming his dog that.

I changed Sappho's name to "Shard." "Swiss Chard?"
people ask. "No. The markings on her body resemble
broken pieces of pottery." I don't go into detail
with dog owners about pottery shards collected
in archeological digs being the main indicators of
history in the male-strewn ruins of civilization,
and that the soul makers of pottery in most
civilizations were women. Shard bares her teeth
to men in uniforms and barks at the rest. I expect
she'd protect me from assault although I've only
once been harassed by a Hispanic male in my
thirteen years of living here. Still, one can't
be too careful/sure these days.

Maybe you'll meet my dogs someday. One will jump
six feet in the air to kiss your mouth, and the other
is known as the Rattlesnake Queen—having been bitten
by one in a gopher hole and kept on digging.

Humanoidads

More than   other boys

The favorite toys of Latin boys de la Misión   are male dolls
G.I. Joe dolls the size of their   fathers' hands   without flesh
blood and substance   The Almost   Touch   of ¡DE DIOS! : hands
and heads come off   the joints screw 'round'a'flurry   !ATTACKMAN!
The plastic surfaces possess camouflaged chameleon properties
labelled Heroid Spy   Captain Turncoat   different shade of
betrayal for every light   y   all these dolls bear weapons
on their breasts

Their fathers in their heads

Young boys of the Mission son preoccupados   momentáneamente
don't demand   ¡Attención!   for "muy mal"   In midst of the
lair of !INFERNAC METLAR! they don't know where   they or their
fathers   are

!MONSTROID DARKSEID DESTROYER!

The boys play with their dolls   more than Latin girls   Ex-
clusivamente!   They draw self-images of Ninjas   interminable-
mente!

!INHUMANOID SHATTEROIDS!

They trade last year's Rambo model in on   this year's karate
master   Ninja ain't bad being veiled   like there's nothing
inside his clothes but   disguised   violence   He kills with
filosofía   and protects inocentes from brutalidades
The veiled male of their fathers missing the boyhood of their
actions   !SECRET WARS OF INSECTOID MANTISAURS mounting CYBORG
SPYDOR STRIDOR STEEDS!

For X'Massman

Fatherless voices of mechanized kids with monotone lips ask for
mansized robots that shoot out evaporación upon laser-proofed
hearts: I.am.Laser.Eyes. a.whirtling.dervish.of.iron.spikes.
and.unshreddable.flesh.better.than.Superman.Mr.T.Goon.Squad.
mentality.and.TV.wrestling.identity

Lackloss

Adulation of Invisible Man es más bombástico than El Camino
Real Auto Dealer   Los Latinitos   go Ape   over Escape and
Missing-Fathers-Bonkers over the presence of a mentally retarded
adult male exiting into perspectivas diferentes

Papá en casa

If Father was around   what might bionics be   The clothes pop
off   weapons eject air full of toothpick expectativas Ah (Daddy
Be Home)   Solamente Latinitas admit Daddy beats on Mommy !POP!

!Pum! ¡Paf!

El Latin boys don't watch where they're going   Niños de padres
que le hacen falta   clutch-stumble along !THE SLIMEPIT OF
LIQUIDATOR MUTORE!   This.is.how.they.talk.how.they.walk   missing
Realidad Street   possessing miniature fathers in their via de la
calle bodies   while their greenless card mother !ENFORCERS! work
in candy factorías and meat-packing plants   to keep the trama-
intriga sons of mystery husbands o masked novios   encapsulated
in G.I. Joeland on !SNAKE MOUNTAIN: EVIL STRONGHOLD OF SKELETOR
AND ROBOTIX D. COMPOSE! boy children until !OPERATION APPENDAGE!
their fingers become !REAL MEN'S! arms and legs AND THEY ARE
MONSTERS de separación!   AXIONMAN! Enmascarados del futuro/
boy children in grown guises transform the everyday Mission into
¡DOMINACION TOTAL DEL UNIVERSO!

Ringing in the Dark

A Clearing Ritual for the Montreal Fourteen

Attempting thinking

Attempting thinking of the complexity of the life of any human
being—joys body functions daily efforts   the caring or lack
the thoughts that stray through the mind *Learnings*

The house that Jack built

In a glade and wooded area in Glen Ellen California a four-story
fortress of boulders and timbers servants quarters trophy and
game room the ultimate male domain the Colossus of the North
went up (how cum) in flames one drunken Jack London night
soon after he'd master-planned it (A gay man has stashed away
personal letters by Jack London of the paranoia of Jack London
crumbling to be touched by a man)

Callings of the Wild a wolf wouldn't touch

The satisfaction of killing a woman who first turned her back
on men because they let her know she wasn't   pretty
*

The cruelty of killing a woman because boys resented her because
she did better in school than they
*

The privilege of killing a woman whose uterus was too narrow
to birth a baby   and who didn't want one anyway
*

The flamboyance of killing a woman who at twenty-five gave up on
men because the man   she gave herself to   kept acting vanished
*

The arrogance of killing a woman who hears music rhyming lesbian
with   separatist

*

The selfishness of killing a woman training to work with young
children   who would have learned eight-year-old boys bond
in clubs while   the girls pass notes on love
*

The spoiledness of killing a woman who would've witnessed
the same boys building a castle—a stronghold with an elongated
drawn-up drawbridge
*

The immaturity of killing a woman watching cardboard additions
to the castle of boys making a cardboard jail   putting
themselves in cardboard bed together   in jail
*

The slyness of killing a woman while the boy-hero looks on in
constant taking motion   the trickster that saps and flags
the careless hard-looker alert-one who never minds   the leader o'
the pack who binds the boys in rivet-action of Pacman pills
*

The impotence of killing a woman knowing girls fantasize
finding a cat or a rabbit or tiger   and taking softness home
feeding it   and it can live there forever
*

The uselessness of killing a woman wearing a man's suit to
ward off men   covering herself with superiormaid cloths of
their deceptions
*

The defeat of killing a woman whose biggest wish is to keep
the land alive   looking out upon the grave of the human race
*

The honor of killing a woman who thinks she's bonded with men
*

The fear of killing a woman in this refuge   den of strength
house that Mama Bear built   keeps men from it
*

Sound a single, gentle chime or bell between each listing.

35

Men Kind

The man returning to the Stockton schoolyard of his youth
shooting thirty-five Southeast Asian children because he claimed
foreigners were taking the jobs He left behind a motel room
littered with plastic toy soldiers

The man kind to his girlfriend 'til mind of her own he didn't
get his way donned army fatigues entered a University of
Montreal classroom in one of any Ol' Boys' departments he couldn't
measure up to and falsely brandished browns yellows & reds
of nature dead leaves heaped up in conflagration The walking
barrage separated the men from the "feminists" "I want
the women!" He lined them up and released the men He uttered,
"You're all a bunch of feminists!" and shot the women then
hunted down more before dismantling himself from his scene

Attempting imagining

Attempting imagining now a young woman who IS no longer
the efforts of parents in raising her her attributes yearnings
tears pride confusions contributions doubts struggles love hurts
laughter tone of voice presence any of us most certainly
each menstrual individual here for Solstice 1989 all that you've
been through your whole life to be here tonight yourself myself
the fourteen women of Montreal Time between each weathering
to attempt to ponder the essence fullness and loveliness of Being

* * * * * * * * * * * * * *

Fourteen intermittent sounds of a chime, finger cymbal or bell.

Christmas Kitty En Bilingualand, Or, What I did this Year

Mision Satánica

I found a
kitten
in the Mission
on the Sabbath.

Gatito negrito
with buttercup
eyes like
pale yellow
saucers.
Who could refuse?

So laden
with fleas,
my milk porcelain
sink spotted with
brujas' blood.

This Halloween
I was an
airline pilot
with a kitty
in the cargo,
hungry as sin,
rescued in
flight on a
school building
doorstep.

I named kitty
"Hallo*ween*,"

the "wee"
or "ween" part
pronounced
with a squeal,
"Hallo*ween*!"
to capture
the misterioso
subtleties
of his feminist-
winning ways.

Kitty Católico

I think
Halloween kitten
is Catholic, for
on Thanksgiving,
he pulled
from the bookcase
a text de religioso:
"The Little Office
of the Blessed
Virgin Mary
and Prayers of
Our Blessed Lady
of Mount Carmel
and St. Teresa
of Jesus,"
teethed it.

Oven's gurgling.
Warmth overlies
blessed frosted
Mission morning
as we say oven's

gurgling warmth
overlies blessed
frosted Mission
morning, and
we said—!Gracias!
for the turkey
Reagan's cooking in,
donated by
Israelis, Iranians,
Contras, Costa Ricans,
etcétera, watered down
to goddess stew.
¡Qué lástima!
Lasting turkey
soup for Christmas!
!Sopa deliciosa
para anarchistas!

Me and the dog
and Christmas Kitty
and fishes tropicales
watch TV winter
proceedings, revelations,
reapings, unwindings,
of Private Wars
of eyeless, lipless,
knows-no, wire-browed,
mouthless men.
I, as author, and
Animals of the Earth
plot BEGINNING HAPPY
ENDINGS BETTER
NEW ERAS!

I Was a Teenage Lesbian, Age Thirty-Five

An Anarchist Response to
a Marxist-Socialist "Three-Way"

I was involved in a three-way once.
The lovemaking perhaps lasted five minutes.
The preparation involved the suggestion
in which my former lover told me her new love interest
who looked a lot like Ms. Liz Taylor—dark, Italian
and gorgeous—wanted to make love with two women
at once.

I was invited over for drinks with them
so she and I could see if we'd feel comfortable
in this love-making arrangement. Trouble was,
Ms. Liz Taylor had a girlfriend she'd lived with
for years who, because of Liz Taylor's
inclinations to wander, was always at her side
to make sure she didn't lose her.

However, on this day, Liz Taylor had managed to slip
away while her girlfriend was at work. Liz had assured
her that she was going to drop by my ex's for
a single drink and wouldn't be staying. A "single drink"
was laughable. The three of us sat with our feet up,
lounging among flounced Italian decor of my friend's
surreal-tasteful waterfront apartment.

My ex-girlfriend was Italian also—not dark—but with
the body of Venus de Milo—but freckled, the mind of
a philosophical panther and the white hair of an exotic
snow leopard. I was a burgeoning writer, intrigued with
themes & variegations on womanly desires. We sat sipping
brandy & wine from our snifters, eyeing the tide and boats
slipping by the bay window, making small talk and getting

decidedly drunk. Maybe half an hour passed and
Liz Taylor indicated to my friend that she liked me;
and I, her. So, blushing, we moved to the bedroom,
growing in anticipation as we pulled off our clothes,
draping them here and there like little anarchic flags
all over baroque-modern furnishings until valances
over yellow windowshades ornate with linings of pompons

bantering at previous lovemaking breezes, sounded.
Sunlight turned the room dark orange—(please explain,
scientifically). Our bodies connected in a circle
on the luxuriously wide bed with tawny lions' patterned
bedsheets. Took some doing, but possible. We
were inside each other's secret fruit, our mouths within
each other's mons veneris. Cantaloupes—tangerines,

I was tasting the bittersweet nib-hardening of Ms. Liz Taylor.
Beyond that, I don't know who did what to whom. A circle's
a simple figure, but who wants to apply themselves to math?
The smell of pomegranates growing stronger, our arousal was
heightening us out of the thaw of booze, when, at the edge
of a rush of climaxes, the phone rang. Simultaneously,
we disengaged ourselves from our clitorises, lifted our

three heads in a gorgon groan of smeared lips. Liz said,
"Oh no, I bet it's her!" My ex: "Hello?" Sure enough.
Venus de Milo handed the fake marble telephone receiver
to the dark starlet: "Hello, Honey... Oh, just having a
second snifter—one for the road. You'll forgive me?...
You're coming here—now? You got off work early—great...
You're going to join us for drinks? Sure, Sweetie.

See you in a jiff." Liz set the lighter-than-it looked
receiver back on its elegant antique hook. "She knows!"
The three-headed gorgon groaned a mighty second time.
Not only did alcohol still have a hold on our bodies,

but the throes of lovemaking had welled us inside
and made us almost immobile. "How long will it take her?"
"She'll be here in five!"

"Lordy!" We grabbed at our clothes and threw them on
and fastened ourselves into a presentable, cursing crew
with a sock or two missing. Who'd look inside our shoes?
One of Liz Taylor's cunt hairs was curled tight around
two of my teeth. I tried to pick at it nonchalantly,
put it in my pocket, a memento. My ex-girlfriend fanned
damp sheets, fluffed pillows, hurried the covers over all.

We didn't have time to comb our Medusa hair or wash
dried white juices off fingers and faces. Liz smeared
lipstick on her where it's supposed to go, without looking
in a mirror. We reseated ourselves in the front room,
our clothed bodies barely reassembled on black & white
imitation leather, our almost empty drinks still positioned
on zebra-striped coasters on askewed Chirico pillar stands.

The brass, lionheaded door-knocker resounded.
Though even this room reeked with pungency of sex, we sat
eyeing each other, nervously hoping to get away with an
afternoon's unreal real temptation. "Come in!" Ms. Liz
Taylor's girlfriend entered in a checkered tweed business
jacket with matching skirt, graciously accepted a drink and
never questioned the air fraught with unstrung shoe laces.

She made polite conversation. The afternoon passed—adieu!
The two women left together. Liz Taylor and her friend
soon moved from the Far North to Malibu, leaving my ex
girlfriend briefly bereft, longing for Liz Taylor.
We heard they opened a chain of gayfood catering businesses
in California, naming their successful operation, "Ambrosia."
(Don't you know gays eat different food than straights?)

Maybe Liz Taylor's cunt hair wound up in some unsuspecting
gay male's stomach and lodged there as a continuous irritant...
Years I've set aside that afternoon's guilty feelings
and decided dishonesty for having betrayed another woman—
though I hardly knew her. Face it: just plain bad behavior.
But, I'd so wanted orange rococo moments—we only had five—
that I did such things when I was young in lesbian love.

In love with lesbian love, I'll never forget that faraway,
shaded bedroom sun, that amber globe bedroom, glowing
midday moon burnishing our bodies with chocolate desires,
our three heads barely treading above watermarks of passion.
When I was young, I wanted what I wanted *so bad.* And when
one gets older—one forgets so easily and yet remembers
O certain moments with total pristine recall.

As for Liz Taylor's cunt hair, I momentarily forgot it and
proceeded to wash evidence of the afternoon out of my clothes.
Even when I was folding them, I forgot to look in the pocket.
But if any lesbian ever finds that eighteen-year-old hair,
it will undoubtedly bring a high price. (I'd certainly pay
a high price for it.) *Perhaps the Gods and Goddesses of Gaydom
are vying for it forever at the banquet table over my head.*

Camille on a Couch

Wilhelmina Dopamina,
that's'a me'a...

People come to her, look
at her eyes, face, walk,
tell her she's in love.
She just looks at them—
the She-Stare of-a-Bear.

Her wedge-pointed shoulder pads'
hint of diamond glint
might eject a sigh.
Forgive her Her Menopause
crouching in corners,

grasping at her shadow,
cloak & dagger-style.
She forgets she's by herself,
by design. Leave her,
leave her be.

Lazarus Lonidier enters
midlife, uttering,
"Everything went right,"
but the perfectionist
keeps dropping things.

Her ever-changing glasses
don't match her intentions,
and her lesbian dentist is
tender-capping vulnerabilities
of her tenderer incisors.

What good is Camille?
You can lean on her
as she faints.
A bit of a vampire—
she would love that.

She enters staged doors
from all sides,
from cracks in drafts,
she thunders in
and doesn't notice

she's lightning
contrast of white
satin & black velvet
and hasn't taken off
her red felt hat

under which is kept
warm stream of a secret meadow.
Ah, pouty Camille on a couch—
sluggish & nauseous, close
as she'll come to pregnancy.

Will she bear a harem
or a siren? Pobre niños.
She drifts over & unfurls,
bumping into fall fashions'
stark looks, or is it

the pining season of non-stop
pinnings on the couch,
she models for?
She smiles. She's got
top-line feminist thoughts.

Ella estudia Español
de progesterone—state of
being eternal in the mouth
of months. Language-jumping
since you took her hand and fully

kissed her, she's forgotten English!
She too is drawn to continental
women who move montañas.
Edificio de Piramide: euphoria
keeps her afloat—

even happy—*and* she's afloat!—
Wilhelmina Dopamina—
Camille on a couch
wishing to be weakened by
a female to advantage.

She enrolls in a
finishing school for women
on How to Succumb on 0
Luscious Points of Another's
Strenghtening Voice of Lilies.

Multicolored changeling,
menopausal—dropping night
veils coursing through her
glowing dreaming on the off-cycle
going nicely wet again.

Fear is, ardor will run
down her legs' replete
return to youth. She'll have
her writing to do over and
periods to live, relive.

People tiptoe up to her,
ask, "Are you in love?"—
Look at her. No answer.
Her widening, narrowing eyes
curl up into the light.

All she holds is
one photo and another's poems.
She's moist-eyed, reciting lines
on a couch past curtain time.
(Some say she's with paper & pencil.)

(None lay eyes on her
at Rilke's merry-go-round at sunset,
dolphin-endorphined and finned,
climbing onto sea spray,
ready to ride.)

Gretel and Gretel
(Recorded by the gamekeeper's daughter)

El Aire Libre

Into the woodsland deep we wandered   dos niñas   lost in greygreen-
'scapes and ever-stretching cabbage patches   a baby rabbit loped
across the road   We rose higher   Forestlight denser

Having been ejected out of your nest   your full-fledged eyes wounded
a dead leaf floated across your vision   and hung at one side of
tus dos arcos iris   like in O'Henry's story   You inhaled clearclean
nerve ends of evergreens   The sky turned rosy-edged blue   embossed
with start of stars   Our talk meteor-showered on every mountain turn:
confessionals   proyectos   dreams   amorosas   dificultades   Twilight
drifted down red-trunked trees' heads-towering reach

Dos picaras - "wandering female trouble-troubamaker-doures"   We don't
trod on the living   We were Gretel & Gretel dropping feminist leaflets
on the path behind us that leads back to men   Gretel and Gretel
proceed

Women Bathing Naked in the Wilderness

In this version las mujeres   are older and therefore   more lovely
their bodies   crisscrossed with wisdom they've journeyed   to learn
Traumerei immerses their limbs in powder pink sulphur moth light
filtered hues de liquid forest runes and pools   A woodsman whose
tool is cutting a path to ruin   strides forth to claim the myth
that's his   No sooner does he enter their realm than the women
turn into lesbians in updraft of swans' beating wings to   Lebenland

Euro-Latin Impersonator Act*

Tú y yo assured ourselves we knew the way *pero* we grew less sure
now that night shut down   except for one gas station and twenty bars
There were no 7/Elevens   or berries *Yes*?

Crickets carressed our pelos de los oídos under accumulating star
clusters and a cut moon   You remembered su abuela demostrandole una
secret mushroom-searching place sequestered from being taken by men

The forest murmurs I want to abscond with you *pero* darker still
the path wound 'round   Hacia el sur? *Yes*?   No   Al norte
Towns and branches' lost feelings of musty roads and dusty views
"You are beautiful—*Yes*?"   We are anarchic Nordic dragonesses
Greta Garbos o Gretels Garbled   La nochenegra Gretel y Gretel evolved
deeper into anachronistic forest hold

*Underscored words are to be read with a lively rise of voice.

Langsam

I had to drive slow to watch for   animals   We'd never get home
You with the patience of learning languages talked to me even when we
didn't need to keep me   awake while you needed sleep

I know that you know that I love you   but I don't know you know that
I fell in love with you on first hearing tus poemas   words so evoked
líneas so primavera   so feeling   so caring so   mind-provoking
they pull sensitive-deep into complexidad y tenderness   Altiplanos
bordering fainting

You are Your Poems are You   I couldn't help be more to you   Arquitecta
de la Heart   than a fairy godmother   ((Yo soy tu fairylover—)) No?

Climax and El Fin of the Fairy Elfin Lovers

¿What was a man at an egg-packing plant doing a medianoche I had to ask
(¡Qué lástima!): direcciónes? We couldn't believe him ¿Trust in
Cocteau's boy motorcyclists pointing the way? The labyrinth dead-
ended in obscuridades totales You asked the time and the way but
your inquiring of kilometers embarrassed-mathed me: How many man's-
sized shoes does it take for women to begin the trek through woods

Our eyes recoiled from duel spectre of lights Nightroad turned
into a two-car accident Committed to getting you back to the safety
of your homemade quilted bed I decided to go on because another car
had stopped to help and I already had an injured victim en route

Gretel and Gretel never did come upon a candied witch's house There
is no witch There was a woodsman— ¿their father long-gone long ago?
This is a feminist version of grim men a lesbian fairy tale without
witches and evil stepmothers with only the two Gretels Handsome &
Handsome

The witch's house is a California oasis with neonred motel signs lining
glimmering palmtree strip called the High Way En esta novela—we enter
the fabled locked door: Gretel & Gretel spinning the nights away tasting
each others' limbs in undying honeycakes swoon They drip sugar for
all that lovemaking keeps Gretel and Gretel from gaining weight
And the thrust chickenbone has been replaced with their lips tongues
fingers swimming in and out of waves' capped crests you call "orgasms"
bursting on chocolatey seacliffs undertowing into caves

Hand-in-hand all the other Gretels in the world went off the path
together hugged and were kissed by leg-shaking moonlight and
found pleasures and meaning delight in This to the belief-shattering
Moreafter Everfor/never-ending Happiness-Day

Greta Garbo Leaves California for Argentina, Not Forever but for Good

(Ode to LavenderRose)

Crossing the invisible

Heading south   Pan Am Airlines leaves Pan Am decals on its
aeroplano   exteriors   Pero   the inside of   "¿qué" (what's)
"pasa?" (happening) at Miami Airport   is suddenly part of a
Borges plot discombobably or disembowingly   strung out as
a B-grade movie trailer   before "take-off"   and *strange*

La interior of the waiting gate   la last-minute check-in desk
el ticket-taker   las attendantes   el gangplank: should the plane
be renamed "Latin-Time Airlines"?   It is 10:45 P.M. boarding time
Five hours between flights I'd caught a Miami city bus driver's
directions to a Cuban restaurant serving   Louisiana gumbo
Greta Garbo disembarked in dark glasses   ate up   and high-stepped
it back onto one of those long-awaited   live-lingual buses

Meanwhile back at L'arena del Sur

The gate's waiting room es   homôngous   Masses of people are
milling about seats suddenly smaller and made of something less
than United States plastic   Pan Am's late loading passengers
It's announced: "Line up according to your seat number"   Which
seat numbers?   Almost everyone lines up   There's so many people
there's   no line   Even in a man's suit Greta Garbo doesn't act
pushy   Stampedes turn on themselves   Have these Pan Am employees
never boarded passengers?

With two heavy carry-on bags and a small styrofoam surfboard tied
to the bottom of one of them I sit   in one of hundreds of

diminuitive seats wondering about   starcluster patterns of
constellations overbeyond this smokey florescent-greenful aura
A few other beings appear as   isolated pinpoints   refuse to glom
with the crowdlings

Greta Garbo wants to be left   to wait

Passed boarding time and three hours beyond bedtime   finalmento-
lentomente   intercom pronounces in dos lenguas: "Now accepting
passenger seat numeros 50 through 70!" *Those* people are already
squeezed in the aisle Finalmentalentamente they get to "40!"
Greta sighs   "30!"   I wiggle my toes alive   Are the masses
being run off the gangway—falling into some Dante-ish airport
netherland   never to reappear?   How they get rid of people in
Sud America?

Finalmentolente "Veinte!"   A last minute surge of people—many
carrying four or five bags   cram onto the loading ramp   Earlier
I spied a small box at the base of an escalator and a tiny handmade
sign: "Don't carry on carry-ons larger than can fit in this box"
No one had seemed to be noticing that box except   "moi"

11:30 P.M. Nordic time

The ramp leading to Patagonia is still jammed   People steer and
shift oversized luggage precariously   Five handbags fall backwards
and almost hit my case carrying a wallet-sized broadcast-quality
stereo-metered Sony tape recorder   Someone ran over my foot with
a wheel of a cart   Fortu-nuttly   Greta Garbo's wearing Her
"L.A. Gear" brand-new heavy-duty white tennies with mini-California
license plate key chain Made-in-Korea   attached   Only the tread
of a cart's wheel left its indelible mark on the canvas overlying
Her proud foot   Whoever ran over us   did not apologize
Mestizos y European Argentinians are not   small people

Next   within steps of an inviting open plane door   the aisle's
jammed with Pan Am employees confiscating tons of excess baggage
out of hands arms and carts of Argentinian travelers and the few
disparate loners   A checker is eyeing my child-sized surfboard
The plane on the USA side had had long narrow cupboards and
'commodatingly received such odd-sized objects   I express concern
over a styrofoam board being lumped in with luggage   I was feeling
smaller   The enlarged stewardess utters: "There's not one inch
of extra space aboard   Pan Am's given us too small a plane tonight
Either we leave people off or we put suitcases where they belong
We can't have both!"

Greta Garble's guess

Every night Pan Am makes too small a plane available to people
heading south   So "Poor Surfboard—adieu!   We'll see   what shape
you're in   in the morning's wash   Will I ever see you again?"
Stewardess-checker assures me they're putting it in the Pet Area
I picture "Pobre Surfboard" in pieces: me drowned at sea   Half
Swedes Indians Argentinians gringas scattered over Amazons

11:40 P.M. a woman in a man's suit Garbo enters a plane packed with
people (Seats twelve-across)   The overhead carry-on racks look
half as wide   as the ones in Estados Unidos   Only thing the same
is the size and surreal twilight of the toilets   Stewardesses
wrapped up in last-minute check-in stuff   One of them's   hunched
on a stool in a narrowest food-serving galley—resembles Rodin's
"Thinker"   hand-on-chin   except   she's sick   Deathbed of menses
'mongst plastic breakfast faces?

Greta's got a windowseat

Gar Goil goes against tide of passenger flow   does the Lambada
overunderthrough   bodies 'til   she reaches *y* opens *Her* overhead
carrier   The carrier's big enough to house three kleenex boxes
The other two seatmates glare at Her as if it were   *their* private
carrier   It's full of a single shaving kit and the other man's
coat   All carriers within reach are jammed full of other *theirs*

My video camera-sized bag might fit under the seat but the larger
bag   a soft bag full of fragile taping equipment: microphone
cable   transformer   tapes   videos   books   a hundred poetry
magazines   has a rip in it and doesn't lock   Reservations
assured me I could carry on one carry-on bag and one over-the-
shoulder bag   No problema

Imagine stewardesses exhausted from the crunch of bodies and bags
being nice   I clasp my surfboard claim ticket   If I get a broken
chunk of styrofoam back   I'm not going to wait for   the rest
I've had that "boogie board" for years   never used it   Greta's
saving it for a night swim with Argentina's greatest contemporary
woman poet (male or female)

A stewardess listens to my pleas for not checking my one suddenly
oversized carry-on bag   "I have a place for it" she whispers
and leads me to the employees' coat closet   Sure enough   there's
a spot on a rack   wide enough to squeeze it in

I'm so sleepy I stumble to my seat   push my one bag left under
the seat   find a pillow with human hairs on it from the last flight
and lean against windowglass   The pilot announces: "We are going
to be late leaving"   (We know that) "Buenos Noches"

Over innercalm comes:

"Our flight is waiting the arrival of two late passengers"   Five
minutes pass   "The two late passengers have still not reached
the plane"   Evita and Juan?   Five minutes to midnight
a pronouncement: "Bags of the two late passengers must now be
located among the plane's cargo"   The pilot reveals annoyance:
"See what happens when someone's *this* late?   We have to wait
atleast fifteen minutes more!"   Greta utters "For Christ's sake!"

In the United States a plane would not wait for a person A person
would wait for a   plane   If planes run late—once a flight's
posted on a TV monitor (even if schedules change)—it's true to
the latest update   USA Pan Am flights leave on time   while babies
cry on board   On this plane   we wait   No one seems upset but me

Babies laugh   Not a single baby is crying—yet   Such waiting is
standard procedure?   Everyone sits and chats   or relaxes   Again
something is said in Spanish over Intercom about the two late
arrivals and their luggage   Either they've located and x-rayed them
(and things)   or Pan Am's finally leaving *them* and *that* behind:
Hearthardy applause   Still   we sit   Intercom asks for this
person and that to come to the front   Is this Argentine soap opera
or performance art?

Many Spanish voices are talking to each other at once   One behind
me   a man   is talking loudly in English with a Spanish accent
about how he was years in charge of twelve people in a bank
He utters an endless array of mundane information you'd know if
you'd never worked in an office   I bet he doesn't know the
combination to the bank's vault   He's talking to be talking
How many people aboard   are doing that right now?   He's bragging
to the totally silent man next to him who either has to hear every
detail of nothing or knows   *not* to listen

12:15 en la mañana

The take-off: one hour late   I feel the plane   start to move
There's the longest take-off—or did Garbo dream it?   The creaking
shaking plane is real   It runs and runs and runs along the ground
like a tricycle   I don't care if we crash   I no longer have faith
this plane is capable of entering   air   I don't care   I fall
asleep (Briefly)

Voices of Panic

In English and Spanish mixed I hear a distinct   "Is there a doctor
on board?"   Calls for a doctor up and down rows   I open my lead-
closed eyes to peep at Pan Am employees   They're standing panicking
right at the seats behind mine   Either the man who was talking
such a streak ('cause I don't hear him now)—or the man who managed
to listen to him—is having some kind of attack

Is there a pilot aboard?   Finalmentalente   a doctor's found and
protests "But I'm not a medical doctor!"   *More* discussion   Perhaps
he's a doctor of education or "see-key-uh-trist"   Both   useless
to the Living   or Dead   At last a stewardess suggests the sick man
may need food   Then intercom announces: "Dinner'll be served shortly"
At after dos horas en la mañana?!!!   The stewardess assures
the sick man that he'll eat first   I picture him rising up   and
with a last gasp   refusing airline food

I struggle   asleep   The man is being fed   A stewardess is
serving my row   I hear her ask loudly "What do you *want*?"   I keep
my eyes closed in disbelief   The last thing I hear her say to the
man next to me is: "Poke her—Ask her if she wants chicken or beef"

Dinner must've lasted 'til 3 a.m.

Estados Unidos airlines leave on time while babies on board cry
Latin-time airlines seem to leave-when-they-leave and ever-arrive
Babies on board laugh When do Latinos sleep? After they eat
Then they sleep and sleep

During this flight I even experienced Patagonia Now I don't need
to go there The man next to me is holding a book entitled that
In reasonable Pan Am morning light we're being pleasant Yes he's
from that remote region of Argentina where Indians remain
ancient and you can barely stand up in wind

The Patagonian gentleman explains our flight had undergone a bomb
scare regarding late luggage arrival and ensuing disappearance
of the two long-awaited passengers And the man with the seizure
was the son of the bank official who talked non-stop That son
happened to be diabetic Because of flight delay and because
he's too quiet (with a father like that) to speak all this
contributed to insulin shock::: why he critically needed food

Hovering over landmasses de Ar-hen-teena

Finally touching earth I was so distracted by the beauty of
Buenos Aires—I forgot about the surfboard I'd received back
in one piece I abandoned it against some hotel lobby wall
or in some taxi's trunk Anyway Greta Garbo arrived at a beach
in Argentina smiling satisfied with a swim in a rainstorm
(sans surfboard) humbled by magnificence and satiated with
difference/between California drought and length and greenness
of these grasses It is said the most optimistic people on
earth this year are Ar-hen-tinny-uns Overwhelmed by different-
but-the-same Nature and Lives—every country has its logic—
I got away with Being Me in Argentina That's liberating
despite contrary history—trials/mistrials

No wonder such big people wanted out of such little seats   as
provided by Pan Am   Not even the foreign rough dark-colored kind
of toilet paper was available at Buenos Aires International Airport
Not a roll or single sheet can be found in its restrooms Men's or
Women's   Greta Gargle checked   There's none: nada nadie nunca
Garbo was glad (and relieved) she'd brought pocketfuls of soft
tissue   white as skins of Fins   along

Female mysteries de Ar-hen-teena

Before playing the cello in honor of newly-arrived Women's Poetry
in this old New World   it's necessary and only fair to announce:
Pan Am's return flight went smoothly   had more room   and left
on time—midnight   At 2 A.M.   a diarrheic wide-awake Greta Garbo
panged with hunger   famished from being moved and touched   and
pockets emptied   ate   wild-eyed contented with the rest of the
passengers   *in awe of Patagonian tunes*   *that're actually German*

*Refrains from "Familien-Gemalde" by Schumann and "The Evening Star"
by Wagner, or similar cello excerpts, follow the poem.*

Una Eternidad

A man is like a tiny dinosaur   thick-headed   small and empty
lots of armor   and feet that crush   and a raveoughness appetite
Think this is glamorous   It's for the fool-hearty   and out-of-
date   Crunch

A toucan en dos macas

Hard-edged TV announcers

Una eternidad of twilights pasearon since el sol pulled up
excruciating heartblues into a thin sky   en su ausencia
O sensia sensual sensual sensitived sensitiva absence you
Yo tu pierdo   Come breathe by me

Rio Blues Set

I woke early in the night from a deep sleep right into the middle of
a blues set   (I'd fallen asleep a la radio)   that seemed to so
pertain to you   and matched my true feelings   that which I was
certain I had succeeded in burying about missing you   the deep arrow
I wouldn't let myself feel

And there was someone good as Bessie Smith   oozing long journeys
of loss   I was drifting in the deepness of my sorrow that I won't
let myself   enter   My sleep pulled into a deep purple ravine that
meandered on and on   And when it was over   the announcer spoke
its name: "That was Oscar Petterson playing, 'Traveling On', recorded

with Betty Carter, on tour in Europe. Recent. Think I'll get this
Real Blues album, desde it got me. Play it again, *missing you.*

La Escribas, Por Favor

I won't write a poem about how you came upon that most famous
11.6-inch clay faience figurine of the Cretan priestess holding
a snake aloft in each hand   You fell to your knees before her
bowed and wept in an European museum where she's housed   Guards
thought you were crazy   Ella esta su poema escribir.

(Also about how you cried in church Católico   "Why?   Why?
What for?"   Tan miraculosa encontrar algunos que sentir cerda de
personas y cosas as intensivo as yo "Despues de cinquenta tres
anos solamente

Because I Was a Late Bloomer

Because I was a late bloomer in the realm of sewing my gay oats
I found myself arriving in Seattle in 1970   knowing no one
hankering for love   hanging out at the women's bars   appreciating
drag shows but madly searching for what   at the time was
inexplicable to myself

I slowly made a few friends   and quickly glommed onto an instant
love who had a high school education—most brilliant mind of my
life and an avid reader in the arts sciences literature and
philosophical realms   and nightly wiped out her eyesight and
consciousness with alcohol

The love affair was just that   the friendship has lasted
to this day   thanks to slightly lower long-distance telephone rates
as   she is still   to this day my beaconing mentor   has remained
in Seattle   is as insightful as ever   a miracle   considering
she imbibes daily

In other words I was craving and searching for wisdom   For me it took
human form in paradox   I have never known a "brilliant" person
from Robert Duncan to Joanna Russ   who did not have some insidious
shortcomings or self-induced handicaps   The most brilliant people
—when I got to know them—are   in some way   extraordinarily

short-sighted   or creatures of some infantile debilitating habit
or constantly annoying behavior   The privilege of brilliance
by those insightful people who baffle   run-of-the-mill   mind-use
folks   which includes the realm of "professionals"   college-
educated or not   has haunted my obsession with "intelligence"

"grey matter"   the "brains" that weight the world   "the world of
ideas" folks   Robert's half-seeing omnihead overweighted with
megalomania   Joanna's non-Hollywood shortened-tendons' beauty
(she didn't have a nose bob) pouncing brilliance and flagging

self-image   and foreshortened memory and prima donna behavior

and memory   if you believe like I believe that ALL BRAINS ARE
CREATED EQUAL—then the aberrations of intellectual and aesthetic
reverance were brought on by enriched early circumstances and
rigid later opportunities rejection and non-understanding in

their formative battles for acceptance as authors by society
These are my protagonists   Robin Morgan equates heroes with
demons   which is not fair   given that all monsters in mythology
are based on actual people who differed from that norm I find
so ugly

'Til Years Let Me Grow Wiser

I am not going to die   nor the ones I care for

I'm not going to die   just like I never get depressed
I'm not the kind that gets depressed   or Karen
But the night I went to the beach was red for Robert
also

Have you noticed the world moving in a movie

While people rare as Robert stand firm in a cyclone   or create
their own   Though I seem to be aging I'm not going to die
Karen didn't   Robert didn't   It's an illusion   a deception
to make everyone think they're everyone else

Scaling cells' replacement

Rules out invidious comparisons   It revolves like a symphony
old-fashioned and remains I stay a child   Not a walking Eastern
sameness-extention   Alan Watts died after all and his neighbor
Elsa Gidlow   but Karen and Robert are here   present at this minute

Cobwebs come upon us

It's a child's game simply to make the world think I'm like it
but I am the same forever alive   You'll see—or maybe you won't

History

Like the flick of a shark-cheating wrist   history is an obscene
flasher   Death is not in the cards   It's a "what-if" situation
a make-believe solution   if there's a single chance the world was made
for one child

If evangelists come looking for poets

We'll disappear into a rabbit hole   world under a heterosexual
village   I'll be an old school marm spinning   I'm not going to
die   you'll see—or maybe you won't see

Like Robert

I grew up young   Like Karen I grew up committed   When singing
evangels commit the young at middle age to institutions   they're
called crazy   Poets survive because they're crazy as queens
exclaiming upon the goings-on in Bugs Bunny Land downunder

When swinging evangels come swinging swords

We'll go underground like mall rats* where we're already there
and goodies are gooey on the trees and good children can do
anything they underworld want

It's not that the sun revolves around us it's not that the world
stands still

At age fifty   people tell me I look thirty-nine   When children
badger I tell them I'm ninety-nine and a half   At fifty I stopped
listening to the news because of Pat Robertson and the blood-
pressure country   Pat Robertson makes Ronald Reagan look
handsome   Pat Robertson is a dimunitive of Ronald Reagan and
logical heir   The poets will live through this age of

It's not that I'm going to die it's just that the world is dissolving
around me.

*teenagers who hang out at shopping centers

Happy Doris on Her '69th

At the announcing of the closing of the zoo
and the libraries and the swimming pools,
isn't 69 one of those classic sexual positions?
I don't mean to imposition or improper you,
but on your birthday they dared announce
they were going to close the zoo.
Where will the peacocks strut their forests?
And who will the gorillas throw doo-doo at?
That's been more fun than the bigger pen
they've been given to romp in.

I loved when you announced you are living
your second childhood. Let me introduce
you to mine: Mexican jumpingbean Ritchie
who does triple flips on the floor.
Xavier with the wavy hair and the Spanish
eyelashes sifting a guilty look
for flushing a goldfish down a toilet
so he wouldn't have to feed it. His mother
in her innocence wonders where's the fish.
Chinese Cindy who thrives on straightening books.
And Alice with a growing voice that doesn't fit
her Chinese: an Alice loud as the Queen of Hearts
exclaiming over cards. Only four of thirty
children—I live with their energy every day.

The dilemma for Teacher me is how are children
going to have books with animals as characters
without animals and libraries on earth?
They'll forget what it's like to be a toad
driving a roadster down Main Street or a pig
talking wonderment to a spider in a web,
without likenesses of animals, without zoos,
without swimming pools.

You have solved such worries for me, Doris,
with your medications tied to your shift stick
so you won't forget to take 'em,
your handheld ratchet (New Year's noisemaker)
and your sausage-making machine. Who could be
more phallic than Pauline collecting all sorts
and sizes of horns with handles attached?
And your red bandana hanky cannot outdo
your honk. You dress and blow your nose
like a man. And I like how you deftly stoke
your potbelly stove with built-in windowglass
called " "* that pearls the flames
that make music sputter.

You stay awake in the quiet night
sampling goldleaf books, taking untantalizing tastes
of Shakespeare, drinking wine, immersing
yourself in mysteries. You sleep in
in the morning, scoop up the news of the latest
closings from your seven a.m. doorstep, read it
and snooze 'til ten or noon.

At poker—you're the most, winning your share,
spelling out every hand, looking up every word:
"poke" "her"—get it? You champion beginners
to win. Ace queen heart spade take my mind
off the vanishing animals and book-stacked
libraries end and evaporating pools. I imagine
you clean winter out of your swimming pool
with classical music turned up full blast.

You are a dream cook. German Swedish Jewish
meat melts in my mouth. The asparagus
lies down with the pears. Thank you for being
so fastidious as to hand me serving spoons
wrapped in paper towels—you're infectious.

You won't kiss on the mouth, and yet you are
Walking Waves of Affection. With your
surgically oiled replacement joints you do a
jig with a dip stick planted in your RV van
with Las Vegas liner lights. You go miles
into woods sounding with lesbian laughter
spread around the camp. Many women love you.
You evade them gently, lightly, kindly.

April birthday, Ms. Fiddlesticks, you make
my pores blossom, and my veins and arteries
are outlined in spring flowers. When sirens become peacocks
in the night, I come to you. Doris, don't
worry about whether you're going to like
this poem or not. They've announced
the closing of the zoo, the libraries
and the swimming pools; I come to you.

Look it up.

Quest

I lived with illusion
I could find a beautiful woman
by writing remarkable poetry.
I had some beautiful women
brief as a season, sometimes
brief as a flower's
singular magenta appearance.

I wanted to live with beauty.
I finally was unable to write
and complained to two women.
One of them who paints spheres
perfectly balanced in space,
assured me I would write again.
The other who is long-time ill, still can make
wonderous depictions with paint.
She has no lover nor is pursuing one.
One could say she's a lover of Nature.

I've always felt the universe is a
beautiful woman, and, without a muse,
I could try a different poem—a mirror imaged
to measure up to a handsome hillside
reflecting the wind combing a grove
of trees—one of Nature's
varied pompadours. How Her hair
tremors! How the limbs hold up
magnificent lady sighs.

I have noticed the spring this year
like never before.
With walks through neighborhood
parks and the richnesses that cover

my eyes in growth in meadows, on cliffs over-
looking the sea, I live with Nature,
and She is unbounding in Her portrayals,
sometimes man-ravaged, always changing
from the tiniest teardrop leaves
(little toes) to the pomade excrescence
of pine pitch. I could try
to attract Her heartbeat with words.
This is new to me and it's working.
It may even heighten realization
that a Van Gogh
was made for the love of the flower,
not the woman.

Lesbian Heaven

All the girl friends you ever went with
are together now, and they're all
getting along. They're lovers of each other,
and you're in the middle playing the lyre
with Greek attire in the middle of a Maxfield Parrish
forest. Doe-eyed nymphs fondling panpipes
while the pure note sounds. Purple mountains
rise over aeolian forests, and the wind
is the pianist for a women's chorus,
and the longest-fingered of all the women
plays the lute. Pluck the chord,
pour the wine. The flute chambers
Egypts of desire. And the glimmer bubble gurgles
of a brook where each stone is smoothed
to the consistency of knees and thighs,
and the sun, a gigantic pearl, livens them.
Lesbian heaven is filled with dogs and cats.
All the pets we've ever had
are tendered by the hands that kept them,
and they all behave—a beloved company
among pillars' uplift and glitter.
Where Diana sets down her hunting implements
and all the lesbians in heaven clamour
to her limbs with tambour touch,
the afternoon unfolds its leaf,
the night cadenzas its embrace,
the stars become the beaded necklace of morning
with the moon as centerpiece.
And the gold of the painting shineth
on me and thee.

II
The Rhyme of the Ag-ed Mariness

A Lesbian-Ecological Opera

THE RHYME OP THE AG-ED MARINESS

A Lesbian-Ecological Opera

Dedicated to Ilse Kornreich,
Valiant Sailor of the Southland

ACT I—The Wake—

SCENE 1—Opening

(Stage with simple setting of a ship with masts.)

VOICE OF AG-ED MARINESS:

A ship moves without a hand
on the steering wheel,
glides as though driven
by loadstar.
As if a hero had named
the ship "Polaris"—
after the North Star—
but no hero came.

"Hero" is a monument of memory.
"Heroics" has its sea burial
over and over, the grim stone
churning ever deeper the waves
brimming crest of waste.

The captain, in sitting position,
leans against the base
of the mast pole on a deck   *(Footage of polluted,*
manned by men propped up   *junk-infested ocean*
as if alive, lying against   *and shore.)*

the railing on either side
of their captain.

Opposite him, at the peak
of the prow, one of the men—
they're all facing his head
bent down with the weight
of an albatross against his neck—

CHORUS *(In hissing, whispered voices)*:

—all their eyes are open, even the bird's,
but nobody sees, no one dreams what lies
ahead for the spectre of ships,
these nailed pieces of wood and metal still
visited by the spirit of heroics
marked by a deed to down a bird—*that* man—
the condition of the birds; his words:
"I shot the albatross because it was there."—
is an image of last gasp—an already given
death throttle *(vocal sound)*
or snake's whorl *(vocal sound)*.

Listen! Hear men roiling over rotting threads
snaked into a pile of rope upon the deck.
Memory of sailors' voices still chanting
to grasp the sea by the hand, so little left
afloat, so little aloft. Men with feet unsettled
as water, yet strive to contain inner cities
of the soul:

(Wagner excerpts, shadows of men and heroics, tumbling and ruin.)

AG-ED MARINESS:

We are tied marvelously   *(Oil-spill footage)*

to a beam of light. The ship
is not driven swiftly by star,
but slowly through oil-coated ooze
that belies the shore.

By the smell of it,
I believe we again pass the banks
of Valdez, Alaska, or is it
the Sacramento River, or just
a blotch of a freeway spill,
a glow-dot mainlining California?
Or East Coast shore lined
with used hospital needles?

We barely move, yet on—on
the timbers creak, boards
beneath my feet sway, the stench
is not just Death but fouler
than downed birds' feathers bemoan
the fate of clinging
to their betrayers' necks
haunted by utterance of what
wonderfully accompanied
the sky once. Centuries
after "The Rhyme," we repeat
its lines, so much more
to cry for now.   *(Footage of living*
                                          Roumanian death camp
                                          victims.)

CHORUS:

Listen and hear chaos of earth at the end
of Earth barely held together by history's yarn.
A shoreline of slim margin, dinosaur slime,
oil on fire at opposite ends of the Earth.

(Visuals from the Middle East war.)

AG-ED MARINESS:

And who am I?—

CAPTAIN'S WIFE *(Appears on deck with mop, singing)*:

Here I am, long passed time
for a ship to sink—the only woman
aboard. I'm the captain's wife.
I stand watch. I swob the deck
and sling the chow. Someone has to
keep this frigging mess going—
and bear the silence of the crew—
never away night and day, fore
and aft, heave, hold sway.   *(Liquid*
I am but a reminder of the figurehead   *of oil spill.)*
of that cursed wooden maiden's head,
breasts and brow blackened
as she parts waves bedecked
with the slick of doom, accused.
As if oil-thick seaweed gripping
her neck were jewelry on
an anchor's chain.

The oil overtakes the sky
turned raven. Stars now are
the jewels and struggle with
their colors. Now even the light
has vanished, the wind is emptied
of sails, absent of its hold
on sails—even it is held in wait.
Not a breath, nor hair wisp blows.
The stars are but holes
left by birds trying to peck

their way through the stern of air.
Only their beaks break through,
taste luminescence of this
moonless night that nods and
turns and twists the ship's bow
straightaway to the sore,
red shores of morning.

(Star imagery dims out as curtains close.)

SCENE 2—Women Stand Accused

(Inside a room with two windows are women in soundless motion,
each with some chosen activity meaningful to her, like weaving,
soldering, writing, picnicing, dreaming, etc. Occasionally,
one of the women quotes an author, breaking the silence of all
their energy with the following three quotes—one given to each of
three women on stage):

> "...the original version of this happiness belongs to a
> category of human being that we can afford to despise,
> to abandon our early respect for, as we grow: The boy
> can start to despise femaleness as he grows toward
> competent membership in the male fraternity; the girl
> can start as she grows toward her love of men, her
> gratitude to him for embodying uncontaminated clear
> humanity, her duty to be his competent supporter and
> assistant, his loyal helpmeet whose desire shall be
> toward him."
>
> By Dorothy Dinnerstein

> "The mother can feel herself the center of attention, for
> her child's eyes follow her everywhere. When a woman
> had to suppress and repress all these needs in relation
> to her mother, they rise from the depths of her uncon-
> scious and seek gratification through her own child...."
>
> By Alice Miller

"The wood resonates. The curtain flaps in the wind.
Water washes against sand. Leaves scrape the ground.
*We stand in the way of the wave. The wave surrounds
us. Presses at our arms, our breasts. Enters our mouths,
our ears.* The eardrum vibrates.Malleus, incus, stapes
vibrate. *The wave catches us. We are part of the wave.*"

By Susan Griffin

(The curtains close.)

SCENE 3—The Captain's Wife Meets the Living

*(Same ship's setting except red sun colors the edges
of daylight.)*

CW: Hey, ho and up she rises
ear-ly in the midnight hour.
Why do I say that? I get mixed up
from the freak weather we've been
having—don't you?

(She listens for response.)

Who am I talking to?—
It's only the hope of someone here
besides me—that I can pour my
soapsuds out to. Way—hey—

CABIN BOY *(From offstage, singing)*:
Way—hey—

CW: Who was that? I believe I heard me
singing beyond myself—as if it
were a ghost. For a long time
I've thought this ship was haunted.

(She listens.) Oh-hey and up she—

CB: Oh-hey and up she—

CW: That wasn't me...
Way, hey and up she rises—

CB: Way, hey and up she comes—

CW: Listen, fallen angel, if you're going
to mimic me, do it right,
or you can't fool me.
I know this ship is steered by daemons.

CB: Demons?

CW: No, daemons, spelled with an "A".
Rhymes with "dames!"

CB *(Steps on stage from forecastle)*:
I beg to differ. "Daemons"
may be spelled with an "A,"
but the sound is "E"! "Daemons!"
spelled with an "A" and an "E."

CW: Well, I stand at attention, corrected!

CB: And what is the difference between them?

CW: Daemons and demons?

CB: No. Daemons and demons.
Daemons spelled with an "AE"
are neither departed souls
nor angels, but rather, spirits
of the air that inhabit space,
are everywhere and keep an eye
on the sufferances of Nature,
accompany Her and guard Her.

CW: This interests me. We've been reading
the same book on philosophy.
The one on Neoplatonic daemonology.

CB: Yes, the one on the captain's shelf
so neglected that, when I picked it up,
the pages gave off dust.
I gave them a good shaking.

CW: The one my husband said he'd read.
So, I read it, and he refused to
discuss it with me. "Daemons,"
spelled with an "AE," speak
in an unearthly tongue and act
as interpreters between gods
and men. *(Aside)*: Somewhat
like women. Closer to angels
than the diabolical—
the better side of men.
The book says "Daemons":
spelled with an "AE" are pre-Biblical,
whereas, "demons," spelled with an "E,"
have horns and hoofs and tails,
do the Devil's bidding.

CB: The Christians gave everything good
a bad rap.

CW: Oh, this conversation is stimulating,
stimulating.

CB: Daemons are known to follow ships
and assume the guise of birds—
much like the albatross.

CW: That makes sense.
Do you know that the albatross
has an almost unbelievable wingspan
of up to thirteen feet?

CB: No. Did you know that "13"
is a lucky number–
the appointed number of women
in a witches' coven?

CW: No, but I've watched an albatross
glide for an incredibly long time,
float on the air directly
above the waves. I rarely see
them now, they're becoming extinct.

CB: I watched a TV special that showed
how they go through
their mating season during
typhoons of winter.
And they can remain at sea
for up to five years without
coming back to land.

CW: I've seen them rest aboard ship.
And for as long as I can remember,
to have an albatross
follow a ship is good luck.

CB: Enough said about albatrosses
and daemonology... And who am I?

CW: By your youth and lively mockery,
–and memory serves me–
you're the cabin boy.
A happy lad and obviously innocent
of this drifting.

CB: I'm the cabin boy but not exactly,
for under these woolens
a far different figure rises.
I take off my hat to you.

CW: You're not a bird,
you're not a ship, you're—

CB: Exactly, I was born female
like you, but don't call me a girl.
I'm a woman dressed this way to ward off
muggers and rapists. And so that
I could get a job doing what I wanted.
It's how I got aboard, passing as a man.
Besides, a sailor suit is more comfortable
and lasts longer than a dress.

CW: You surprised me, but
none of the others aboard
will mind because they seem to be
in some kind of trance.
They're in limbo, yet their eyes are open.
Besides, the ship itself is cursed—
moves by itself.

CB: Interesting.

CW: I like that you're using that word.
As god-awful as events on this ship
have passed by me, I find them
interesting though I haven't been
a part of them. And though
I should bemoan the fate
of these men here, I have held on
from the distance of an observer,
not a participant. But actually,
it's become almost unbearable
to see life around me quickly ruined.
It ain't entertainment.

CB: Talk about being a part of history
without participating in the shaping,
I too have been horrified,

yet fascinated with the foolishness
and folly of men. Enough so
that I dressed up and passed as one.
Even learned to spit like one.
But you're right. Things have gone
too far. When life is only a memory
of the living, and the living
are enlivened only by the groans
of a death throe—

CW: Tell me what it's like.

CB: You've been living testament
to a dying ship too.

CW: Not that. I've had too much of that
already. What's it like to be
a cabin boy?

CB: You talking about the tasks
at hand?

CW: No. What is it like to dress
as a man?

CB: Tell you what.
Any one of these men here
can afford to lose his suit,
since they're not alive,
even if their eyes are open.
So I'll just strip one of them.
Relieve a sailor of his togs
and you can try them on.
(Looking about.) Here's one of
suitable size. If he's alive,
he'll protest the removal of his
jersey and bellbottoms.
See, he doesn't move.

(She bends down behind the forecastle.)

CW *(To herself, a soliloquy)*:
I must admit I've always wanted
to pull on those high-button pants
and reach into the heavy sleeves
of a p-coat and stand with my legs
bowed, do a jig, pull on the rigging
of this ship and train it
to sway with my fingers' tug,
do my bidding. Climb to the crow's
nest, get a glimpse of distance.

CB: Here you are. You want me
to turn my back?

CW: Naw, What's to hide?
I like the idea of you watching.

CB: So do I.

*(CW slips into sailor clothes. CB helps her button all
the buttons and straighten the suit. CW throws her dress
offstage. She looks at CB as if CB were a mirror image.
CW mimics CB.)*

CW: Would you like to be a man?

CB: No. The longer I was a cabin boy
and witnessed first hand what I saw
in men, the more I was glad I was
female.

CW: Are we in imitation of men,
of how it is to be a sailor?

CB: Not exactly. Sailors, yes—
but a different kind of sailor.

CW: You know what I would like to do?

CB: I know what I'd like to do.

CW: I would like to sail the sea
as one of those different kind
of sailors.
See the world, take things in
both good and bad.
See the world for what it is...
And what is it you'd like to do?

CB: Kiss—

CW: you. *(CW plants a quick kiss on CB's mouth.)*

CB: No, no. Kiss as two women would
as if they're lovers.

(CB reaches over and kisses CW long and passionately.)

CW: My, that's a fine start
for a long journey!
Now who will steer the ship?

CB: Well, in your attire,
what role do you want to assume
on our trek?

CW: Do we have to play roles?

CB: No.

CW: All right, then I will.
I've—I've always wanted to be
a dike.

CB: A dike, huh?—and I, a femme.
So take the helm.

84

I'll take a turn later.

CW: We'll take turns.
Which way shall I steer?

CB: South.

CW: Yes, because the men steered North—

CW &
CB: —and got us in this predicament.
We feel a breeze now, an actual wind
seems to have ruffled up from our words.

*(Foam and waves are projected on the boat as it moves
more swiftly now. The curtains close.)*

Act II—The Maidens' Voyage

Scene 1—Men Stand Accused

(Not a sound on stage. The setting consists of the women who enacted different activities in Act I, Scene 2, now standing motionless in different poses and stances in a desert-painted backdrop. A couple tall cactus plants are used as stage props. Every woman wears the same gorilla face mask made from a paper cut-out from a photo of a gorilla mask. The gorilla women stare at the audience. The curtains close.)

Scene 2—House of Coatlicue

(Both women are at the helm; it's twilight; they each have a hand on the helm and a hand holding each other. Their eyes are upward.)

CB &
CW: Lie down, my love,
 lie down, facing up
 so that you can count
 the stars, and so that
 my outline—the outline
 of female can be on top of
 female.
 Side by side,
 we take turns
 reading the stars—
 a kind of lovemaking.

    AG-ED MARINESS:

The Archer becomes Diana.   *(Stage darkens. Star*
Hercules becomes her snakes,   *patterns of two histories*
not of power but of existence,   *overlie each other.)*

Taurus becomes the cow
of an earlier time.
Orion the Hunter—
the animal he's clubbed
becomes the Albatross.
The Albatross is the burden of
believing in a fixed system—
(We just changed that).
The bright stars of Orion's girth
become the kindness of a fusing
instead of a disjoining.
And Virgo the Virgin and Crater
the Cup are nuns spending
nights together spinning.
The Milky Way stays milky.
Star clusters moving in on themselves
become Goddesses—an earlier time—
and the dippers become double axes;
the axes become butterflies, and Orion
the Hunter becomes the House of Coatlicue

*(Apparition of the Aztec goddess appears in day-glow colors
in the dark.)*

CHORUS:

Coatlicue, the Aztec Goddess named for her skirts
of snakes. Two-headed, opposing, monstrous,
created by men, She can split her skin to an earlier
time, to the layers of what she was: a wise woman,
a kind woman—when the spinning nights of a gentle
touch of a woman's hand—sistrum—sistrum—
the musical instrument of this woman's earlier time—
sistrum—sistrum—when women were decision makers—
sistrum—and were listened to—sistrum—sistrum.
They say, "It's a stage." We say it's the way
it is with women taking care to birth and restore
and an occasional gentle man occasion accompanies her.
Hear the Goddess herself, Coatlicue...

(Coatlicue opens up to reveal an ordinary woman inside who emerges from the colorful apparition.)

COATLICUE (*Singing*):

I sing the song of myself, the same one, only deeper,
sung. My history comes from drawings on bowls
burned by Spanish sacrificial priests in 16th C. purges
and bulldozed by 20th C. treasure hunters.
Yet from the Southwest and Mosoamerica pieces of me
survive—why I am able to sing fragments of my life.

I am of the Gran Chichimeca. In 1050, figures standing
around with bows and arrows and incense gave my vagina
teeth. Before that time, I was a comfort to enter
and leave without harm, like slipping in and out of
the moistened softness of a plant burgeoning
dewy flower petals.

Quetzalpetatl was the Catholic Church's first
creature of demon proportions, and her song,
the vagina dentata, was left out of Man's recordings
except for an oversized mouth or an unnamed woman
whose hips measured seven hands across.
And Itzpapalotl who became flint who became fire

was first the goddess, was just a woman who became
the terrible mother who spoke Spanish, the men said,
who initiated human sacrifice and war, the men said,
ordering them to shoot their arrows in all directions,
and she went underground. Men wanted her that way.
Her vagina became a devouring mouth.

The obsidian butterfly eats men. Believing this,
pre-Columbian priests ripped the victim's heart out
and part of the thigh and threw the body away.
The male priests there raised the corpses and
thought of them as the goddesses' leftovers and
attributed such eating to me.

To them I am not werewolf but an old woman who
is actually a weredeer. They say she chases them
in the shape of a ghost. Or two old women
with hair as white as maguey fiber, committing
adultery with some young men. Does this speak
for the unsatiability of women with men?

As for the men... a quote from the Mayan Bible:
"...if you have become impotent, if you no longer
arouse anything, what other purpose will you serve?"

Scene 3—Morning Light

*(Night sky has changed to Amazon jungle morning. The
goddess has disappeared.)*

CB: Ah, light opens my eyes to a forest floor
so thick I can only see four feet
in front of me. That is all the further
I need to be, my love by my side
the night through. We reached out
to each other and held one another
firm and soft under the moonless stars.
And heard the rainbow color
of an ancestral goddess prolong
the bright. She was like an orchid.
This forest is like the sea.
Our touch upon our skin was ecstasy.

CB &
CW: We do not need men.

CW: I come out of a sleep
deep into the centuries.
There stood a figure singing to us
in the dark as we made love.
She was like an orchard.
So certain were her colors vivid,

yet plain she was to take my breath
beyond that already heightening play
of ours.

CB: I thought perchance I dreamed
a woman sang to us last night
of ancientness, methinks,
and antecedency.

CW: Yes, with clarity amongst
a lot of bleeding.

CB: There was mention of blood...
 Menstrual?

CW: No, nor menopausal... Victims,
 and age...and advantage.

CB: And ascendancy.

CW: Limbs of the Goddess—

CB: wrap around...

CW: This must be the Amazon.
 Entanglement of sunlight
 entwines the soul, awake.
 Looking into our ancestry,
 this is the house I feel I know,
 though I've never lived in it.

*(Superimpose slide
dissolves of the Palace
of Knossos at Crete
onto Amazon jungle.)*

CB: How could it be? The vines
 clear across the ocean
 hold the buildings in place,
 winding a trail to the heart—
 a collaboration of goddess,
 labyrinth and horns.

CW: The path of the jungle
becomes a dance.
A single-file configuration
through two mountains:

CB: breasts suggesting rest.
The procession of priestesses,
wings raised, arms aloft,
an architecture of femaleness,
a bathing ritual center.

CW: This is the house I feel I know,
though I've never lived in it.
Tunnels and funnels
and echoes of caves.
A patio uplifting to a hill.
An open woods,
a building in the shape
of the body of the Goddess.

CB &
CW: There is consensus in our
reading that this is the way
things were... and are...
and ought to be.

CB: Here, the steps lead down to light.
Here, men and women take turns
grasping a bull by the horns
and riding over its back
to land on their feet, upright.

CW: There was no killing of bull,
but a glance, a jostle with Nature.
An earthquake is a glimpse
of adjusting one's balance to Hers.

CB: And through the ritual center
ran water masterfully contained

in its direction down to baths
and passages out. The fluidity
of buildings themselves
spoke of Her.

CW: To quote the noted author:*
"...the site expresses engulfment
by the earth afer leaving the sea
and the palace is a forecourt
for the fertile Mesara."

Scene 4—The Plant Gatherers

(Scene slowly fluctuates between Amazon jungle and leveling of the jungle throughout the length of this scene.)

AG-ED MARINESS:

Man as Scavenger

Botanists brave the jungle,
now climb trees, risk their lives
gathering millions of plants,
drying them between newsprint
put to use. They label and study
remnants of verdure, the obsolete,
the replete, the almost extinct,
and store them in an herbarium.
These kinds of plants would have
made medicine for Man or just plain,
precious air.

CHORUS:

The Amazon is downed at a mile a minute by slash
and burn and buzzsaw. The limbs of the maidens
of Greeks are cut off and drop resounding

92

as pottery shards upon the rainforest floor.
Clink, clank, plunk—crash! They disintegrate.

AG-ED MARINESS:

A ritual from the Zuni Indians—
the sealing up of vials,
the closing of the nipple lip
is sanctified. To the Greeks,
the first bowl was made in the shape of
a woman's breast.

CHORUS:

Half the rainforests have disappeared,
the rest will be felled in fifty years.
With no winter to discourage insects,
there is only a thin layer of foliage
on the soil, it decomposes so fast
from heat and moisture.

CB: We can't keep pace,
we can't keep track.
I read the trees lack rings
for they grow year-round
and can't be dated.

CW: In a book, the word "Amazon"
means "moon-woman."

CB: Who knows but that the Amazon
was named for its trees
stretching larger than life,
holding anacondas, toucan
clickings and kinkajou chitterings
in its centuries' limbs.

CW: Dearest, look now.

What a mess we have here,
from giant trees to cattle deep,
the de-greening of the land
to parched earth and dead straws.
A cow raises her head
and the moon cries out—
a new moon, a scythe.
Don't call it for what *they*
saw it as—an emasculator.
Beyond the forest,
the only thing levelled
is the cow.

CB: Honey, it's a horned crescent,
a harvest moon shield over
the Amazon. Women warriors.
Minced meat. They claim
she was named for lopping
off one breast so she could
aim her arrows better.
Shall we follow her decline
down the forest 'scape
of moisture? Shall we aim
the skeleton ship of
drying bodies down
the evaporating river
to a sea of cattle
brought to their knees
by cleavers?

CW: Whatever, we seem to be
scaling the planetary twilight
with the moon.

CB &
CW: It's because we love each other
and *it* so—this jungle birth
of myths, this tiller of
the body of ships set upon

a glimpse of green,
a tide of hope.
We're still at sea.
The leveling of the rainforest—
rainbows into meat patties—
a jungle curse.

CB: Not a curse. A curse
is put upon you.
This is Man's curse put upon
the earth itself by Him.

CW: Let us align the ship
with the disconcerting,
discontinuing Isthmus of Hope.
After all, albatrosses mate
during typhoons at Cape Horn.
The biggest storm lies ahead.

(The storm grows. The curtains close.)

—Intermission—

*Honeycakes in the shape of vaginas
are served at a refreshment stand.*

Act III—Strange Sights & Wonders

Scene 1—The Watch

(The two women on board ship embrace.)

CW: We touch ships of other women
alive in our time. A schooner
far smaller than our vessel
stands before us. It's all-women's   *(Footage of women's*
crew is running a race to win   *team preparing for*
the America's Cup.   *America's Cup race.)*
It's said they're not strong
enough to man this sailboat—
they haven't a chance to win.
Who cares if they win?—
and they may. Truth is, they're
doing what no other women have done,
proving it doesn't just take
male strength to draw the ropes
and pull the jib and time
the landward haul and count
the knots and slick the hawser
through hawseholes.

CB: We cruise ships of other women   *(Footage of men*
in different seas. A vessel   *boarding the supply*
larger than our ship brought food   *ship brought by*
and medical supplies for the people   *women's groups to*
of Kuwait, capitol of Iraq—Bagdad   *Kuwait.)*
in an earlier time—and site
of a recent archeological find
in the shape of the body of
the goddess—an early goddess-
worshipping people.
The Middle-Eastern War surely
slowed down the uncovering

of discovery, even jeopardizing
such find. This boat of
Women for Peace was brought
to a standstill before it reached
shore. It was searched by men
from the West, prevented
from landing; the cargo in the hold,
confiscated. The women aboard
beat their breasts and called out
their protestation in Middle-Eastern
cry. In the wilderness beyond
the sea they were called traitors.

*(Women on stage and backstage beat their breasts and shriek
at the top of their lungs. Stage lights cut to total darkness.)*

AG-ED MARINESS *(In the dark)*:

There's no twilight in the tropics—
it's light to dark so fast.

CHORUS *(In the dark)*:

When people say "people" but mean "men" for
the worst human behavior... When people say "people"
but it's really women who network and bond
internationally... When women are isolated in
the jungle, nurturing... When someone or something's
being taken care of, the odds are there's
a woman afloat.

Scene 2—Women's Mysteries

AG-ED MARINESS:

It is a Mediterranean night in
the olive orchard. The priestesses

have brought sistra of Isis to the orchard.
A sistrum's curved shape resembles
the lunar orbit.

(The stage gradually receives moonlight.)

A sistrum is a spinning device of a single
wooden ball made of elements representing
the four directions, against a wooden
cage, the handle of which is held during
ritual processions. It wards off evil.
The sistrum is a women's musical instrument—
through centuries of disuse, which herein,
is revived. It's used to stir up dust
and decidedly resembles sounds of bees
in an orchard bright. Diana carried it
and so did Hecate. The latter's version
was that of a gold circle with a sapphire
center twirled by oxhide thong. Here
it was used to reveal hidden things.

*(Women slowly and ritualistically appear on stage lead by
priestesses. Each priestess is spinning a sistrum, the sound
of which intensifies electronically. Each sistrum may be lit
by tiny lights also. Each priestess is dressed in a floor-
length, gold, flounced skirt and has a high hat on her head,
resembling a cat. Each priestess is bare-breasted or wears
an imitation resemblance of breasts. Other women carry tree
branches and set them into bases on stage, or are lit up by
leafiness of trees projected on stage. There is a large cloth
snake—the size of a fourteen-foot python—passed by shoulders
from woman to woman in a processional dance-step as the
priestesses gradually leave the stage but continue the sounds
of their instruments into the distance as the dancers begin to
slip into the night.)*

Scene 3—A Wash

(The two women grasp each other in silence as high waves tip and wash over them.)

Scene 4—A Shore

(Daylight. CB and CW stand on land marked by tree branches.)

CW: It all has disappeared.

CB: What—the ocean? Not really.
It and the ship are here beside us.
Feel the fog dot the air?

CW: When we landed,
my dreams slowed down
to the pulse of shore.
You must have noticed
how the shore stops our
heartbeats speeding to beauty.
I feel uneasy, a wavering
like waves taken over
by the immensity of events.
I feel afraid, not of demons
but of men. We now stand still
in the wash of one of the most
cruel times on earth. Even ashore,
I fear this ship's reign
on my life. That somehow
we'll be made to pay as if
we were at fault for the condition
of earth and men here.

CB: But the ship let us off
with the ease of a single foothold

on land, as if Nature, Herself,
held back the wind and waves
and set us here and paired us.
We need not atone
for the actions of men,
including the killing of the bird.
This wounding of Nature
was not our doing.

CW: It's as if Nature made us
into partners. We were so much
like one voice, so in accord,
we didn't differ in where
we steered the ship.

CB: We simply shared the direction
the ship took.

CW: Such case frightens me—
the complexity of such relating
made simple.

CB: To have such harmony is rare
but possible, as evidenced.

CW: We were of the same voice
but it was not monotonous.
It was revealing, renewing.
But I feel your being
younger than me, perhaps
I took advantage of you—
out of loneliness and despair.

CB: Don't bring age into this.
I could just as well say,
"It's generational—
your expressing guilt over
love of a woman"—but I won't.

CW: Perhaps I am.
Methinks we got involved too soon,
and you have been my captive,
being that I'm the dike,
I'm like a man. Perhaps
I dominate.

CB: *(Smiles knowingly to audience.)*
Sweetheart, I'm not certain
I would've taken this journey
without you, and it's been
without regret. Unlike a "femme,"
I could've walked away.

CW: Not easily. We were at sea.

CB: Why the continuing disquiet?

CW: My being a captain's wife,
I've been too long at sea.
I'm made insecure by land.
And I was certainly stuck
in a place of aimless drifting
when you came along. But now
that we're back on land,
people might see us and think—

CB: The unthinkable?..
our lesbianism.

CW: Yes, I've been used to what
people think, and at the same
time, I don't care. In this case,
I'm feeling guilt for what I
haven't done. I haven't been
what I want to be.

CB: And what is that?

CW: You'll laugh. I want to be
a woman in man's pants.
I've done it at sea
but not on land.

CB: You haven't changed out
of your sailor suit—
you're being that right now.

CW: Yes, but your voice is lower
than mine. You can pass
as a man. With my waistline,
I can't. I've looked in a mirror.
My waist is too wide.

CB: So are many men's
and women's waists.
Don't be vain.

CW: Vanity must be a carry-over
from my captain's wife days.
Not that I was a raving beauty
with a mop for a dance partner.

CB: We'll go places where women
will accept us as we are.
Through history, many women
have lived like they wanted to.
Some paid a price,
but it's worth the freedom,
don't you agree.

CW: Agreed. It was an amazing
dream of a journey.
Such sights and wonders
as we saw.

CB: The more reason to travel
together. There's much to be done

on land to help the sea,
to work on ecology. I have
to have faith our race with
the end of the earth will turn out
meaningfully, and that we must
relinquish this fleshly-rotting
ship with her out-of-date crew.
Remember at the Cape how twice
around she turned and was
submerged, and yet we hung on
while bodies in limbo fell apart.
And still their odor hovers, now
that bodies have gone past limits
of resurrection and decompose.

CW: When my husband was along,
I was overly stressed by land.
The sea is not haunted by spirits
but by the smell of spoil.

CHORUS:

Women encompassed by inertia of the male
vision to ressurect heroism.

AG-ED MARINESS:

That said, the ship appeared to disappear.
The sails became dead leaves.
Wood became driftwood. And in place of
the twelve men aboard, like magic or not,
eleven seagulls and one overly-large
gull—the oversized captain—
sat on the waves. Accompanying them
was a second huge bird, which appeared
to be the albatross. They rode the waves
a ways and then flew off.

CB &
CW: We are changelings tied to beliefs.

That's what gives us doubts
that the planet can be saved
...and hope. Changelings in the tide.

CB: Remember at the Cape, how we
rolled around like babes in cradle,
in waves higher than the hills' calm
surrounds us now? We were
wonderfully diminished into
the inconsequential.

CW: It means "being brought up to height
by Nature."

CB: Or "down to Nature."
Here we are staring at Brazil
from down under. Whichever
way you look at it.
Perhaps you're reliving women's
lot in life again. Dreaming
and blaming oneself *are*
women's lot in life.

CW: *(Laughing.)* Oh, "Lot."–You mean the man
in the Bible whose wife
turned into a pillar of salt
for showing interest in wickedness
and sin?

CB: Only incidentally.

(The two women laugh together and hug.)

I mean that which makes me
glad I bear men's clothes
on my breast and rest
my head in books by women.

CW: Being?

CB: Kate Millets *Sexual Politics*,
Marilyn French's *Beyond Power*,
Sarah Hoagland's *Lesbian Ethics*,
Sonia Johnson's *Wildfire*,
and many others.

CW: Could I borrow them?

CB: Thinking I had no one
to share them with,
I left them behind—
save for one that I picked up
at the last port. It's not
a book but a magazine without ads.
It's *Ms.* magazine. newly reissued.
Yes, I'd love it if you'd read it.
Then we can share what
each of us thinks about it.

CW: Beloved, show me now.

CB: Here, I happen to have it
in my inside pocket.
We'll get to the books
I've stored in trunks ashore.
We'll travel North and visit
women assisting others in
jungle regions, Latin cities
and U.S. deserts. I know
two women who are together
in an alto plano region.
There they rediscovered an
irrigation method used
by the pre-Columbians to bring
crops to people who formerly
knew the land as too arid
to work. We can visit there first.

CW: *(Opens magazine.)* Mmm—Robin Morgan,

Andrea Dworkin, Alice Walker
and Joanna Russ—hmmm?
I'll give *Ms.* a try.

CB &
CW: What land have we stepped on now?

AG-ED MARINESS:

The southern-most tip—the land below
The Goddess of the Agave—the woman
with 400 breasts...the Century plant.

CHORUS:

In a time for women to be not upstaged but
be upstage to form Hecate's circle of lights
the crown of lights is joined
to the albatross. She is King and Queen
and nobody at all. She is One. She is Female.
'Tis gold being returned across oceans
to the riverbed of the Rhinemaidens.

(Stage dims quickly to total darkness.)

Scene 5—"Plasmar"

*(An electronic circle of spinning lights is brought on stage
in the dark.)*

CB: We'll add a cross to the circle of lights.

CW: A Christian cross?

CB: A far earlier cross—
a cross of musical spinning
without advertisements.

The Egyptian ankh, Isis' sistrum,
the pagan cross.

*(An electronic cross is brought on stage and positioned
with the circle of lights to form the female symbol.)*

AG-ED MARINESS:

A ship is like the rolling stones of Patagonia,
whether it be the Mediterranean temples of Gggantija
on the Isle of Gozo or the stone balls of Patagonia
in Argentina where the sea swells to a tempest at the tip
and sailors retell the tale of the "Ancient Mariner"
for the first time, as if it were virgin, where
round rocks roll giant stones around in shaping
the Body of the Goddess, where natives now refer
to those rock-cut tombs as "Witches Houses."–
They're ours to claim.

CB &
CW: The albatross whose path
flows like violincellos...
(Cello solo starts.)
...the soaring albatross of thoughts,
our unity through centuries
pinpoints the lights of our journey.
The albatross is the crossroads
of our minds, whose head is fastened
to our souls' softness, hearts
of musical intent. Did Emily Dickinson
quote an albatross? The albatross
as prophesy? The albatross
revives, lives on.

AG-ED MARINESS:

The Spanish word for this is
"plasmar", meaning "life flow", "song".

(Cello solo ends.)

CHORUS:

In this same place—same earth's proximity where
the wind gives birth and blows you over,
where masses of children and other family members
disappeared in the red hot of slaughter
in Buenos Aires where the protestations of
the voices of the Mothers of Plaza de Mayo
changed a government, call out like thunderheads
in a lightning storm, cap and overlie clouds
in rainbow namesake of humanity, we leave
the two women where women increasingly touch
across continents, continuing their exploration
of alliances, each other and the earth.

(Pause)

*(Recording of two of the Mothers of the Plaza is played in
Spanish with English translation above. Slide close-ups
of their faces are cast on the scrim. This is followed
by the electronified sound of light passing through the
female symbol of lights as the curtains close.)*

1981

1972

1972